This text was first presented
as a television meditation broadcast
over the Trinity Broadcasting Network.

Destined for the Throne

"A new theology of prayer." "I have read every book I can find that has ever been written on prayer since the first century. *Destined for the Throne* is the greatest of them all." "*Destined for the Throne* has meant more to me than any other book except the Bible."

Don't Waste Your Sorrows

The author views the adversities in the life of the believer as a valuable part of God's training program in preparation for the throne. "If we suffer, we shall also reign with Him" 2 Timothy 2:12.

Love Covers

A viable platform for Christian unity. The greatest sin of the church is disunity. Fellowship between genuinely born-again believers should be on the basis of a common origin, a common parentage, and a common relationship rather than a common opinion or theology.

Destined to Overcome

"For we wrestle not against flesh and blood, but against principalities, against powers, against the rulers of the darkness of this world, against spiritual wickedness in high places" Ephesians 6:12.

This message deals with the tools, weapons, and "know how" to wage a successful warfare. "To him that overcometh will I grant to sit with me in my throne" Revelation 3:21.

SPIRITUAL WARFARE 2

DESTINED FOR THE CROSS

Paul E. Billheimer

President Emeritus
of
Great Commission Foundation, Inc.

Tyndale House Publishers, Inc.
Wheaton, Illinois

Acknowledgment

I am deeply indebted to many sources. I owe much to the works of John Wesley, Alexander Maclaren, Stuart Holden, J. R. Miller, A. B. Simpson, Amy Carmichael, Watchman Nee, and many others. The Holy Spirit has used their insights and some of the beautiful language gleaned from their writings to stimulate my spiritual imagination.

I relinquish all claim to ownership of any Spirit-inspired truth. All of my brethren, including all members of the Body of Christ, are welcome to use any part of this message, subject only to the terms of the copyright.

My sincere thanks to Norma Aspin for her dedicated assistance in typing these manuscripts. Also to my wife for her valuable suggestions and many hours spent in proofreading and correction.

Seventh printing, May 1986

Library of Congress Catalog Card Number 82-50436
ISBN 0-8423-0604-8, paper
Copyright © 1982 by Paul E. Billheimer
Printed in the United States of America

Contents

FOREWORD 8
PREFACE 9

PART I
Come Down from the Cross

1. THE THRONE OF THE UNIVERSE
   IS A CROSS 13
   The Law of the Universe Is Self-Sacrifice
   Satan Offered Christ a Crossless Conquest
   This Truth More Than Historical
   The Battle Begins
   The Battle Intensifies
   Binding the Sacrifice

2. HOW ONE COMES DOWN FROM
   THE CROSS 19
   The Cross, the Secret of Victory
   Even the Legitimate Must Die

3. HOW TO USE THE CROSS 22
   A Deeper Death to Self
   Not One Way for Christ and Another for Us
   The Cross Is the Death of Indulgence

4. A FATAL ERROR 25
   The Cross and Authority

5. PROGRESSIVE DEATH 27
   A Crisis and a Process
   The First Word of the Gospel
   Repentance and Restitution
   Sick Enough to Die
   The Cross, Both Substitutionary and Representative

6. SIN, BOTH AN ACT AND A
   DISPOSITION 31
   The Pathway to Life
   A Battle Royal
   Even the Best Self Must Die

7. TRUE HOLINESS—A BALANCE BETWEEN
   EXPERIENCE AND ETHICS................. 34
   Holiness and Self-Promotion
   True Holiness Is a Balance Between Theory and
      Practice
   Holiness Is Not Theological Correctness
   True Holiness—A Balance Between the Crisis and the
      Process
   The Decentralization of Self
   The Truly Holy Soul Has No Personal Interests to Serve

8. THE GLORIFICATION OF
   MARTYRDOM 39
   We Are Expendable
   Patriots Are Expendable, Many Christians Are Not
   Communists Are Expendable, Many Christians Are
      Not
   Christianity's Lost Note of Heroism
   Was Christ's Death a Waste?
   The Law of Life
   Death in Life Or Life through Death

PART II
"As Dying, and, Behold, We Live"

9. LOOKING AT THE NEED 47
   The Necessity of Firm Purpose
   The Price of Spiritual Progress
   The Apostle's Challenge
   Unbroken Men of Little Use
   We Die to Live
   No Life Except by Death
   The Corn of Wheat
   The Broken Alabaster Box

10. WISDOM OF FORGETTING 53
   The Purpose of Grief
   The Danger of Grief
   The Blessing of Sorrow
   Don't Waste Your Sorrows
   Forgetting Our Mistakes
   Mistakes May Become a Blessing

God Can Overrule
If At First You Don't Succeed
As Seemed Good to the Potter
The Pathway of Repentance
Forgetting Our Hurts
Forgetting Past Attainments

11. THE SLOWNESS OF THE PROCESS 61
It is God Who Fashions Us
Nothing Accidental
God Is Not Done with Us Yet
This Is Not the Devil's World

12. CONCENTRATION 66
Envy of Angels
Lowly Tasks—Heavenly Grace
A Step on the Stair
No Effortless Sainthood
Devotions by the Clock
Practice Makes Perfect

13. THE VEILING OF THE FUTURE 71
The Veiling of Heaven's Glories
"As Thy Days, So Shall Thy Strength Be"
A Day at a Time
Shoes for Rough Roads
Life's Finest Gold
God Guides the Planets
He Also Guides Human Lives
He Guides His Little Ones
He Guides by Little Things
Earth's Crammed with Heaven
He Guides through Commonplace Things

14. WHAT IS YOUR MISSION? 79
Cheated in Life?
Think of Christ's Lowly Sphere
God's Ways Are Right but Not Always Smooth
Paul's Uneven Pathway
Beauty out of Darkness

15. LIFE IS NOT ALL ACTIVITY 84
Time Spent in Sickness Need Not Be Wasted
The Importance of "Rests"
Every Life Needs Its Winters
God Is Beating Time
Devotion before Action
Priority of Devotion
The Korean Prayer Mountain

Foreword

As a teen-age student in a Christian college, I had the privilege of listening during daily chapel services to many of the well-known "deeper life" speakers of those long-ago days. And though I was anxious to understand and act upon their messages, I failed again and again—year after year—to catch the meaning of their sincere and oft-quoted biblical admonitions to "Reckon ye also yourselves to be dead indeed unto sin . . ." (Romans 6:11). Just as I had received Christ by faith, so too, I was told, I could be released from sin's power within me by faith. But for me, it didn't work. I reckoned and reckoned but nothing happened except a lot of years of failure and discouragement.

How I wish I had had this book in those days. How much spiritual suffering it might have saved me. For here are brought together the Bible's full teaching on this vital subject, with instructions about *what to do* to put faith into action and to test the self-deceit that can so easily destroy the attainment of the goal.

Our author points out that "what we have done theoretically" (to reckon ourselves dead to sin) "has to be practically wrought out in all the endless varieties of daily life. . . ." And he tells us how.

He points out, too, something else that I discovered early—that it isn't easy to continue to desire to be crucified with Christ. Here too he gives us invaluable help that can "allow the Spirit of God to stay on the throne of your heart instead of following your natural desire to run your own life—into a spiritual ditch."

I hope this book will be as exciting and helpful to you as it has been to me.

Ken Taylor

Preface

The message of this book, which highlights the **progressive** work of the Holy Spirit in the life of the believer, is especially dear to me. Although I was reared in a deeply spiritual home and heard preaching and teaching on the work of the Holy Spirit from my earliest recollection, yet I had never comprehended that the work of the Spirit in the believer is twofold, i.e., both a crisis and a process.

I feel sure that no one ever spelled it out this way, but my understanding of the work of sanctification or the filling with the Holy Spirit was that in that marvelous crisis experience all of my nature and disposition and characteristics would be so mightily cleansed and transformed that I would be all but glorified. I thought that from that point forward, my life would be one angelic panorama of perfection. But I was never able to achieve such an experience. As I look back over those years, I feel sure that there were times when I did make a full commitment and consecration, and the Spirit did meet me with His assurance of acceptance. I was full of joyous anticipation of a wonderfully changed me. But in a short while something unlovely which I despised in myself would show up, and I was shockingly disillusioned. At such times I did one of two things: either I threw up my hands in defeat and often near-despair, or I went ahead professing the experience of sanctification with a guilty conscience. **I had no idea that there was a way to meet such defeats with victory.**

It was not until a few years after my husband's marvelous healing from tuberculosis when he was at the point of death, and we were again ministering in the pastorate, that the Lord began to give him insights and he began to preach along the line of the **progressive** work of the Holy Spirit **after** the crisis of sanctification or the filling with the Holy Spirit. I was jolted awake. Maybe, **just maybe** there was a way out of this awful "merry-go-round" sort of spiritual existence I had known for so long. At that particular time I was in the state of "professing without possessing" and I was so miserable. How I longed to be delivered from this awful life of defeat and guilt.

One Sunday morning I knelt at the altar as a seeker and began praying for a genuine deliverance from this awful bondage of repeated hope and despair. I was determined that this vicious circle of wretchedness in my spiritual life **had** to come to an end. There was much learning as well as confessing, repenting, and restitution to be accomplished. I continued to be a seeker for a period of two full months. I am sure that many people grew weary of seeing me at the altar in practically every service, but I was determined that there **had** to come an end to this horrible existence.

I think that part of my problem at this point was the idea that when the Spirit came, there would be a mighty, emotional demonstration that would convince everyone that I truly had received Him. Most of all, **I wanted my husband to be convinced and have confidence in me.** I think that was my **last** point of "dying." My hunger became so great that while resting one Sunday afternoon, I said to the Lord, "Lord, I am so hungry for Your presence that I will accept just **any** kind of an evidence. I will accept just a Scripture." What better could I have asked for? Inwardly I heard Him say, "If you will get up and get your Bible, I will give you one." I jumped to get it. **Here is what He gave me:** 1 John 1:7—"But if we walk in the light, as he is in the light, we have fellowship one with another, and the blood of Jesus Christ his Son **cleanseth us from all sin.**" Hallelujah!

That was more than fifty years ago and that promise

still speaks to me. It has unfolded and expanded all through the years. I was to see that the active verb is in the continuous present tense. That means that as I keep on walking in new light with which He Who is Light illuminates my faults and shortcomings, His blood **keeps on cleansing me.** It was my husband's preaching of the message of this book that the Spirit used to illuminate my "evidence" verse, and the blood of Jesus has kept on cleansing and still cleanses after more than fifty years.

Beloved defeated believer, please search this message and let it search you under the guidance of the Holy Spirit, and the "blood of Jesus Christ will keep on cleansing you."

Mrs. Paul E. Billheimer
February 1982

PART I
"Come Down from the Cross"
CHAPTER ONE
The Throne of the Universe Is a Cross

THE LAW OF THE UNIVERSE
IS SELF-SACRIFICE

Self-sacrifice is the foundation upon which the universe is built, the law by which it operates. If sacrifice were not the supreme law of the universe, would God, the **supreme ruler** of the universe, operate on that principle? Through **Calvary** God is saying to us, **"This** is the throne of the universe, not only for Christ; it is the only pathway to power, authority, and rulership for everyone."

Satan challenged this principle and lost. In all the circumstances of daily life and practice, God is giving each of us the choice of acting on this principle in preparation for eternal rulership—or, of **coming down from the cross** in self-saving, thus losing the crown. The only people who have genuine authority over Satan are those who choose to stay on the cross, allowing it to deliver them from all self-seeking, self-serving, and self-promotion.

Matthew 27:39-42—"And they that passed by reviled him, wagging their heads, and saying, Thou that destroyest the temple, and buildest it in three days, save thyself. If thou be the Son of God, *come down from the cross.* Likewise also the chief priests mocking him, with the scribes and elders, said, He saved others; himself he cannot save. If he be the King of Israel, let him now come down from the cross, and we will believe him."

Luke 23:35—"And the people stood beholding. And the rulers also with them derided him, saying, He saved others; let him save himself, if he be Christ, the chosen of God."

SATAN OFFERED CHRIST A CROSSLESS CONQUEST

At various times in our Lord's life and ministry, Satan offered Christ an easy pathway to supremacy, or to power without the cross. But as often as these offers were made they were refused. Jesus deliberately chose the cross. The temptation and opportunity to escape the cross were ever present during His career. But He set His face like a flint and even finally precipitated His own death.

At the very beginning of His ministry, Jesus faced this alternative. "All the kingdoms of the world and the glory of them will I give thee, if thou wilt but fall down and worship me." This was an offer of a deathless conquest, of a crown without a cross. Indeed the whole force of the temptation lay in the prospect of **power apart from suffering,** of **elevation without humiliation.**

The same alternative was presented to Jesus in the visit of the Greeks who said to one of the disciples, "We would see Jesus." It is thought by some that the Greeks intended to ask Him to come to their country, where He could continue His work in safety, free from the threat of death. And Jesus met that invitation with the words, "Except a corn of wheat fall into the ground and die, it abideth alone: But if it die, it bringeth forth much fruit." Christ knew that His death must precede an extension of His life to the heathen world, and He refused to be sidetracked.

A third time He met this temptation. While they were on their way to Jerusalem near the close of His ministry, Jesus told the disciples what would happen to Him at Jerusalem, that He would be mocked, spit upon, rejected, and crucified of the chief priests and scribes. To the fleshly mind of Peter this would be a tragedy and result in the nullification of His entire ministry, to say nothing of the frustration of Peter's ambition to become a power in a temporal kingdom. He, therefore, took Jesus and began to rebuke Him and to say, "This shall never be to thee." Again Jesus refused the temptation, saying to Peter, "Get thee behind me, Satan."

In the scene before us Christ hangs upon the cross. His prophecies about His death are upon the point of fulfillment. In this dread moment His anticipations are fully justified. The hour for which He came into the world has struck—almost, but not quite. Once more, in the agony of crucifixion, in the awful throes of death, in the last moments of agonizing pain, the temptation reappears, "If thou be the Son of God, come down from the cross."

It is not necessary to say that Christ had the power to do so if He had chosen to use it. "Thinkest thou that I cannot now pray to my Father, and he shall presently give me more than twelve legions of angels? But how then shall the scriptures be fulfilled, that thus it must be?" Matthew 26:53, 54. This He said to Peter in the Garden. He could have come down. And the temptation was sharpest to save Himself and evade the cross in the hour when He was draining the very dregs of the bitter cup of Calvary. With His pulses racing and the fever raging, with every nerve and muscle an agony of pain, with the sense of abandonment crushing Him, the taunt, "If thou be the Son of God, come down from the cross," came with terrible force.

Will He come down? Will He answer the challenge to save Himself? Will He finally refuse the cross? The throne of the universe is at stake. If He comes down from the cross, He will lose the throne. For strange as it may seem, here is where Satan was finally defeated, completely undone, and cast out of his seat of authority. As Dr. F. J. Huegel says, "The world's throne is a cross. Christ reigns from the tree." Because He went to the cross, today Christ is supreme in the universe and that supremacy will one day be openly manifested as the book of Revelation clearly teaches. **Remember, beloved, there is not one way for Him, and another for us.** This is a satanic deception.

THIS TRUTH MORE THAN HISTORICAL

All of this is purely historical. Christ reigns today because He went to the cross and stayed there until death released His life unto the world. But it is more than a historical truth. It is moral as well, for Paul says, writing of believers in Romans 6—"Knowing this, that our old man is crucified with him, that the body of sin might be destroyed, that henceforth we should not serve sin." "Therefore, we are buried with him by baptism into death: that like as Christ was raised up from the dead by the glory of the Father, even so we also should walk in newness of life." "Planted in the likeness of his death." And in Galatians 2, "I am crucified with Christ: nevertheless I live; yet not I, but Christ liveth in me: and the life which I now live in the flesh, I live by the faith of the Son of God, who loved me, and gave himself for me." These Scriptures and others teach very clearly that all believers share in Christ's death. But as Dr. Huegel points out, our death in Christ is **a potential communion.** He says, "Though from the divine viewpoint it is a thing long since consummated, historically and objectively completed, yet from the human angle, it is something held in trust for us, which only upon the exercise of faith becomes effective, in experience."

THE BATTLE BEGINS

When we consecrate ourselves wholly to be sanctified, cleansed from the carnal mind and filled with the Spirit, we agree that our "old man," who has been judicially crucified with Christ, shall be actually and practically nailed to the cross. When God sees that we mean business, that the consent of the will is really genuine, He accepts the sacrifice. **And then the battle begins.** What we have done theoretically has to be practically wrought out in all the endless varieties of daily life, Christian experience, and conduct. Once we agree that our "old man" shall be actually and practically nailed to the cross, a great hue and cry is immediately raised by Satan, who begins to sympathize with all the life of nature and of self, just as Peter sympathized with Jesus when he said, "Lord this shall never be to thee." And unless we are very careful, we will accept the sympathy, agree with Satan that our flesh must not die, that we are too good for the cross, that in our case the cross is a mistake. Sympathy is a very subtle thing, and while it is often a Christlike trait, it may also be of the flesh. Jesus refused Peter's sympathy, saying that it was of the flesh and not of God. He knew that His throne was a cross and He would not be turned aside. When God is dealing with someone in discipline, when He is letting the cross work in a life, be careful how you sympathize with him. You may be taking sides with him against God. By such sympathy, you may indeed **draw that person to yourself**, but you may draw him away from God.

Satan will always do everything possible to prevent your going to the cross in full consecration for the death of your self-life. When you have made the initial surrender to allow the cross to slay your "old man" of the flesh, he will do everything possible to get you to come down, as he tempted Jesus to do. He may have some Peter or his brother to say, "This shall never be to thee." Oswald Chambers says that "no saint should interfere with the way God disciplines another saint." He calls that being an "amateur providence."

THE BATTLE INTENSIFIES

As soon as you surrender your "old man," the old life of nature and of self, to be practically nailed to the cross, Satan or his instruments, like Peter, may begin to sympathize with all the life of nature which has not yet practically gone to the cross. And while what we call the carnal mind, that which rebels against God, may indeed be slain, so that the whole being desires only the will of God, yet as each individual experience of new and deeper participation in and application of the cross arises, the temptation is always present—"Save thyself and come down from the cross." And although we have yielded ourselves to be crucified, when it comes to individual instances of practical application of the cross, who is there who will dare say that he never yields to the temptation to "come down from the cross"?

BINDING THE SACRIFICE

While a great many people know what it means to take the position and commit themselves to the cross in a crisis of consecration and faith and to experience the consciousness of cleansing from the carnal mind, very few of us who are so-called sanctified believers and holiness professors know what it means actually **to live the crucified life.** There is utterly a fault among us on this point. And for lack of teaching on the daily and progressive application of the cross, for lack of teaching on moment-by-moment living the crucified life, we holiness professors have for the most part **remained shallow and immature.** After you have yielded initially to go to the cross in full consecration for time and eternity, it may require real determination to resist the temptation to compromise your consecration and come down from the cross. Psalm 118:27 urges this kind of resolution: "Bind the sacrifice with cords, even unto the horn of the altar." This does not sound like a picnic. **For lack of emphasis upon the crucified life, our Christianity is sadly lacking in depth.** Not realizing that the sanctified life is nothing less than a life of **ever-increasing participation in Christ's death,** we have, in unguarded moments, come down from the cross. Instead of majoring on a life of crucifixion constantly maintained by deliberately refusing to come down from the cross, **we have depended upon a past crisis.** And when we have realized evidences of the flesh, instead of taking them at once to the cross by confession and restitution, we have merely pointed back to that crisis and said, "Since I have been sanctified, there can be nothing more in my life that needs the cross. I am through with the cross. I died once and I am through with death." **And that attitude is the mother of a whole brood of spiritual vices as ugly as they are numerous.**

CHAPTER TWO

How One Comes Down from the Cross

Perhaps by this time someone is saying, "Just what do you mean by coming down from the cross?" My answer is, **"any saving of self** is a coming down from the cross." Any taking of an easy way where spiritual principles are involved is a coming down from the cross. To be explicit and exact: **All efforts to excuse, defend, protect, vindicate, or save self is, in effect, a coming down from the cross. Self-pity** is coming down from the cross. Self-pity is a form of self-defense. It means that you think you have been wronged and you are sorry for yourself because you cannot do anything about it. When you give in to self-pity, you have come down from the cross. **Submitting to resentment** is a coming down from the cross. Resentment is self-defense. It means that you feel that you have been wronged and you are peeved because you cannot do anything about it. **Self-vindication** is a coming down from the cross, for vindication is a form of self-defense. What troubles have resulted from efforts at self-vindication! Whole churches have been torn apart and souls have been damned because someone could not refrain from seeking to vindicate self. You have to come down from the cross in order to vindicate yourself. Vindication is self-defense. **Refusing to accept blame and placing it upon others** is coming down from the cross. You know how hard it is to be blamed for something and how easy it is to throw blame on others. That is a form of self-defense and is a coming down from the cross. When one is misunderstood, undue efforts to explain oneself is the same thing. We have not the faith to do as Jesus did: commit our souls unto God as unto a faithful Creator. **Self-justification** means that we have come down from the cross. **To take offense at a real or supposed slight** is to come down from the cross. **Most, if not all, unkind criticism is a form of self-defense** and self-justification and is, therefore, a coming down from the cross. **Party spirit,** which is nothing more than rooting for my spiritual group or point of view, resulting in a definite reflection upon the intelligence or sincerity of all who do not agree with me, is only a subtle form of self-justification and saving of self.

I think no honest and informed person will dispute the statement that almost all of these things, if not prevalent, are at least common in practically every holiness denomination and many so-called Spirit-filled churches. I will agree if you say that even worse things than these prevail or are common in many large denominations, but that does not in the least justify toleration of these things in our midst. It only proves what I have been saying, that although multitudes of us can witness to having been saved and sanctified, or Spirit filled, very few of us would dare to say we are living the crucified life.

THE CROSS, THE SECRET OF VICTORY

And yet right here is the secret of victory: **not a past crisis primarily, but a present, day-by-day yielding to the cross. There is only one place of power over Satan and that is the cross.** It was on the cross and by the cross that Christ overcame him. The cross was his undoing. **And that is the only place where Satan is ever defeated. The only time that Satan cannot touch us is when we are upon the cross.** The only part of our nature that Satan cannot touch is that part which has been crucified and **remains on the cross.** If you will look back on your own life, the only time that you have been defeated was when you came down from the cross. **And you have always been defeated when you were induced to come down from the cross.** If Satan could have seduced Christ to come down from the cross, he would have overcome Christ. **And Satan always overcomes us when we**

come down from the cross. If Satan can get us to come down from the cross, he has us in his own power. But he cannot touch us while we remain upon the cross. That is where he was defeated. The cross is his undoing. He can have no power over us while we are upon the cross, but we are overcome when we come down. And we continue to be defeated until we go back upon the cross. **The cross is our only place of safety. It is the only place where we have power over all the power of the enemy.** Not knowing this, many of us who have had a definite crisis of sanctification or the filling with the Spirit have not known how to use the cross as a weapon against Satan. We come down from the cross, take things in our own hands, follow our own judgment, fall into self-pity, self-justification, resentment, and other forms of self-defense, and suffer defeat until we give it all up and agree to go back to the cross. We shall find constant victory when we learn to stay on the cross.

EVEN THE LEGITIMATE MUST DIE

Some people reject my emphasis on progressive sanctification because they believe in sanctification as an instantaneous work. **Nothing that I have said is in the least degree calculated to question that position.** I am only trying to put an **ethical content into the profession of sanctification** which I believe is greatly needed today. And I am not the only one who feels that way.

The cross is not only for sins and sin but for our legitimate self as well.

CHAPTER THREE
How to Use the Cross

That there is a legitimate self as distinguished from the carnal self, some of the best writers on holiness agree. The cross is not only to put away that which is in direct contradiction to God, which we call the carnal mind, but it is **to remove also all the life of nature and of self**, which could not come under the classification of rebellion against God, which nevertheless, since it belongs to self instead of God, cannot be used of God and must therefore be set aside. George D. Watson, a writer in the early holiness movement, says relative to this point:

A DEEPER DEATH TO SELF

There is not only a death to sin, but in a great many things there is a deeper death to self—a crucifixion in detail, and in the minutiae of life—after the soul has been sanctified. This deeper crucifixion to self is the unfolding and application of all the principles of self-renunciation which the soul agreed to in its full consecration. Job was a perfect man and dead to all sin; but in his great sufferings he died to his own religious life; died to his domestic affections; died to his theology, all his views of God's providence; he died to a great many things which in themselves were not sin, but which hindered his largest union with God.

Peter, after being sanctified and filled with the Spirit, needed a special vision from Heaven to kill him to his traditional theology and Jewish high churchism. **The very largest degree of self-renunciation, crucifixion, and abandonment to God, takes place after the work of heart purity.** [Emphasis mine] There are a multitude of things which are not sinful, nevertheless our attachment to them prevents our greatest fulness of the Holy Spirit and our amplest cooperation with God. Infinite wisdom takes us in hand, and arranges to lead us through deep, interior crucifixion to our fine parts, our lofty reason, our brightest hopes, our cherished affections, our religious views, our dearest friendship, our pious zeal, our spiritual impetuosity, our spiritual arrogance, our narrow culture, our creed and churchism, our **success**, our religious experiences, our spiritual comforts; the crucifixion goes on till we are dead and detached from all creatures, all saints, all thoughts, all hopes, all plans, all tender heart yearnings, all preferences; dead to all troubles, all sorrows, all disappointments; **equally dead to all praise or blame**, success or failure, comforts or annoyances; dead to all climates and nationalities; dead to all desire but for Himself. There are innumerable degrees of interior crucifixion in these various lines. Perhaps not one sanctified person in ten thousand ever reaches that degree of death to self that Paul and Madame Guyon and similar saints have reached.

And I would like to add that they reached these deeper degrees of death to self by means of the cross in its daily wearing aspects. It is very easy to wear the cross around the neck or on the clothing without practicing the death it symbolizes in our daily personal relationships and attitudes. That is where it really counts.

NOT ONE WAY FOR CHRIST AND ANOTHER FOR US

If we want God's best for our lives; if we want increasing power and victory over sin and self, we must come to terms with the fact that after we have been born again and filled with the Spirit, **we are still fallen beings.** We need to understand that there are large areas of our lives and dispositions which must be continually yielded to the cross and death if we are to live triumphant and victorious lives. This is what Paul means in Romans 8 by the term "walking after the Spirit." In order to do this we must accept the cross and allow it to continue to slay the flesh. According to *The Living Bible*, in Galatians 5:24, 25, Paul says, "Those who belong to Christ have nailed their natural evil desires [the life of nature and of self] to his cross and have crucified them there. If we are living now by the Holy Spirit's power [filled with the Spirit] let us follow the Holy Spirit's leading in every part of our lives." **This indicates that the Spirit's conquest of our fleshly nature is not necessarily automatic. We have a choice in the matter.** We can decide to refuse the cross way, the way of brokenness and self-crucifixion. And that means defeat. **Our only place of victory is on the cross. Christ reigns from the tree. There is not one way for him and another for us.** He went to the cross not only as our Substitute, but He went there as our **Representative** to show us that the cross is actually the only place of rulership.

The cross is not only for the death of sin but for all the life of nature and self as well, even the so-called good traits of that life. And this is why George D. Watson calls for a deeper death to self. **God wants continuously to remodel us.** When we let the cross do its work, God will make us all unlike what we are now. Some of us think that is impossible, but that is why God permits the cross in our lives, that is, those things that keep on slaying our self-life. Our refusal of the cross is the reason for so much friction in the home, in the church, in commerce, and in industry and labor.

THE CROSS IS THE DEATH
OF INDULGENCE

The cross is concerned with our lifestyle. Is an elegant and luxurious lifestyle of God or the flesh? Prosperity is indeed a part of the gospel, but it is only one part. The overall emphasis in the gospel is without doubt upon a sacrificial way of living. **The cross is the death of indulgence.** The cross will make one sensitive to his responsibility to a lost world. There is enough in the

Word to encourage faith for every need (Philippians 4:19), all that is necessary for efficiency. **The use of material things for more than this is luxury and promotes indulgence.** It is said that in his first year of full-time service, John Wesley lived on an income of twenty-eight pounds. Although God prospered him with an ever-increasing affluent work, it is said that he continued to live on that same income for as long as he lived. **I believe this is a biblical standard of stewardship.** "Then said Jesus unto his disciples, If any man will come after me, let him deny himself, and take up his cross, and follow me" Matthew 16:24.

CHAPTER FOUR
A Fatal Error

What shall I do when I realize I have come down from the cross, when I have suffered defeat by taking things into my own hands, by falling into self-pity, resentment, or otherwise into acting from self or the flesh? Many people do not know how to use the cross. When they experience failure, they have a bad time. Immediately their crisis of sanctification is called in question and they have a fierce inner struggle over the genuineness of their crisis experience. If after examination and prayer they finally decide that their crisis was so pronounced that they cannot doubt it, they gradually recover from their distress and go on. **But they have not dealt with the relapse which caused the question to arise.** They have assured themselves that they are sanctified and that therefore they must be all right, when as a matter of fact the Spirit does have a controversy with something in their lives. Too many people go on the assumption that if they can conscientiously say they are sanctified or Spirit filled, there can be nothing more in their lives with which the Spirit has to deal. **And that is a fatal error. It results in the habit of hiding behind a past experience instead of dealing with dispositions with which the Spirit does have a controversy.** And is there anyone who in his honest moments will not admit that even though he has had a genuine crisis experience he still may realize dispositions which are displeasing to God? What should one do with those dispositions? Take them right to the cross. As soon as you realize you have come down from the cross and have suffered a defeat, however small, instead of trying to prove to yourself that you are sanctified and therefore all right, realize that you may have been filled with the Spirit **and yet there is a thing in you that is not all right.** The Spirit has a controversy with you. You have relapsed into the flesh of your self-life. Realize that you have come down from the cross and go back to the cross. **Give up your rights if that is what you have contended for; give up your resentment or self-pity or self-saving.** Die to the thing that caused you to come down from the cross and you will find yourself in victory again.

THE CROSS AND AUTHORITY

How do you go back upon the cross? You go back upon the cross **by confession and restitution.** The evidence that your crisis experience was genuine is not that you never again fall below your best but that when you discover your failure, as soon as the Spirit reproves you for your defeat, **you are willing to humble yourself, acknowledge your weakness, mistake, or sin, accept full blame for it yourself;** if others are involved, request forgiveness and make restitution if needed. As you make a practice of this, you will find increasing victory over your weakness and your defeats will be less frequent. In the opinion of some spiritual leaders, an advanced degree of the graces of the Spirit may be even more important than the spectacular gifts of the Spirit.

This is not to discount the importance of the gifts. But the absence of the graces of the Spirit may counteract or nullify the blessing of the gifts. Failing to yield to the cross in its daily application, refusing to live the crucified life, may be fatal to the operation of either the gifts or the graces. Refusing to come down from the cross is basic to the exercise of spiritual power. **The cross is the only place of authority**. No soul moves toward God without satanic opposition. All the forces of hell are mobilized to prevent any Godward move. Only an awakened and deeply convicted soul can overcome this opposition and then only by the help of the Spirit. If your problem has been the overprotection of your rights, remember that the only right a genuinely crucified soul has is the right to give up his rights.

CHAPTER FIVE

Progressive Death

Earlier in the series, reference was made to George D. Watson's remark concerning a deeper death to self. This seems to some to be a misnomer. If a person is dead, can he be or become any more dead? In the natural world of the animal or vegetable kingdom, this could not apply. But in the spiritual life, death to the life of nature and of self does seem to be progressive. **Growth in the life of the Spirit is gained at the expense of the flesh or soulish life.**

A CRISIS AND A PROCESS
The life in the Spirit is entered by crisis, a crisis of death and resurrection, but is continued as a process in which there is an ever-deepening experience of union with Christ's death. We hear very little about a

crisis of death to self and the world as a prerequisite to entering the life of the Spirit. **We hear a great deal about how simple it is to be saved or to be filled with the Spirit.** There is an element of truth in this but it is only one side. It is easy when we have faced up to our cross and given the consent of the will to die. Each deeper death results in a more glorious resurrection. As far as I know, Jesus never withheld the cost of discipleship. In fact He exhorted people to count the cost. You remember that He insisted on this in Luke 14:25-35.

THE FIRST WORD OF THE GOSPEL

Recently on TBN's "Praise the Lord" television program, Dr. J. Edwin Orr pointed out that the first word of the gospel is **repent.** He made a survey of several groups he addressed by asking them what they considered the first word of the gospel. Everyone should know the answer but not many of them did. It is easy to accept Christ and be saved after true repentance. But no one can be saved without it. Jesus is the authority for this. "Except ye **repent**, ye shall all likewise perish" Luke 13:3. It was Jesus who explained that there was joy among the angels when a sinner **repents.** Repentance was the first word of the gospel as spoken by John the Baptist. To the scribes and Pharisees he said, "O generation of vipers, who hath warned you to flee from the wrath to come?" Repentance was the first word of the apostles on the day of Pentecost. During Peter's sermon when the multitude said, "Men and brethren what shall we do?" Peter's first reply to this was, **"Repent"** Acts 2:38.

REPENTANCE AND RESTITUTION

What does the Bible mean by the term "repentance"? Perhaps the best known definition is "turn around." That sounds very simple but it may not be as easy as it sounds. For repentance involves first of all a **conviction of sin.** In Acts 2:37, while Peter was preaching the Word, it says that they were "pricked in their hearts." Real conviction of sin brings a sense of condemnation. The convicted sinner feels that he is under God's judgment and is in danger of eternal punishment. **Real conviction of sin is followed by godly sorrow for sin, confession of sin, forsaking of sin, and restitution for sin.** Restitution means making right, as far as possible, the wrongs one has done to others. If one is not willing to do this, it reflects upon the sincerity and genuineness of his repentance. It is doubtful if saving faith can be exercised without genuine repentance. When repentance is full and complete, faith for forgiveness and salvation comes easily, almost automatically.

Not everyone believes this, but I believe that there is also a preparation to receive the life of the Spirit. That is sometimes called consecration or commitment. In earlier times it was called a "death," death to all the life of nature and of self.

SICK ENOUGH TO DIE

In order to enter the life of the Spirit, one must become sick enough of this old self-life really to die. There is an old consecration hymn upon whose wings many seekers, in years gone by, have been borne into the fullness of the blessing. It has been almost forgotten and lost to the Body:

Oh, God, my heart doth long for Thee;
  Let me die, let me die;
Now set my soul at liberty;
  Let me die.
To all the trifling things of earth,
They're now to me of little worth,
My Savior calls, I'm going forth;
  Let me die.

Lord, I must die to scoffs and jeers;
  Let me die, let me die;
I must be freed from slavish fears;
  Let me die.

Unto the world and its applause,
To all its customs, fashions, laws,
Of those who hate the humbling cross,
  Let me die.

When I am dead, then, Lord, to Thee
  I will live, I will live.
My life, my strength, my all to Thee
  I will give, I will give.
So dead that no desire shall rise
To pass for good, or great, or wise,
In any but my Savior's eyes;
  Let me die, let me die.

THE CROSS, BOTH SUBSTITUTIONARY AND REPRESENTATIVE

It is true that Christ has already done everything for us. It is true that He "paid it all," but the cross is not only substitutionary, it is also **representative**. Initial life in Christ is entered by a death route and that is not easy. "Know ye not, that so many as were baptized into Jesus Christ were baptized into his death?" Romans 6:3. The life in the Spirit, sometimes called sanctification, is also entered by the death route. "Knowing this, that our old man is crucified with him, that the body of sin might be destroyed, that henceforth we should not serve sin. For he that is dead is freed from sin" Romans 6:6, 7, that is, to live a life of holiness as suggested in verse 18. "Being then made free from sin, ye became the servants of righteousness."

CHAPTER SIX

Sin, Both an Act and a Disposition

Most theologians consider sin as both an act and a disposition. Sin as an act can be and is forgiven in justification and the new birth. Since you were born with the disposition to sin (Psalm 51:5) and are not responsible for it, it cannot be forgiven but must be cleansed. Many theologians teach that this cleansing begins at the time of the filling with the Spirit, sometimes called sanctification or the baptism with the Holy Spirit. **But sanctification, which begins in a crisis experience, is also progressive.** This is where the deeper death to self comes in. In Ephesians 5:18 Paul exhorts us not only to be filled with the Spirit but to **keep on being filled.** Alexander Maclaren says that all along the pathway to increasing holiness or likeness to Christ we will have to set up altars upon which the life of nature and self must die. He insists that the pathway to loftier spiritual beauties will be stained with the bloody footprints of wounded self-love.

THE PATHWAY TO LIFE

None of this sounds too easy. Death is not a pleasant subject but it always precedes, and, when the conditions are met, is followed by, resurrection. In the spiritual, as in the natural (John 12:24), death is the pathway to life.

Is it important to emphasize death as a prerequisite for the filling with the Spirit? Death is a forbidding subject. In focusing upon it we may be accused of being sepulchral. **But are there no conditions involved in the receiving of the Spirit? Is there no preparation to make?** While the Spirit is received by faith, just as salvation is, **are there no conditions for faith's exercise?**

In the book of Acts it seems that the Spirit was frequently received by the laying on of hands following instruction and prayer (Acts 8:15-17; 19:6), and sometimes following instruction only, as in Acts 10:44. In the light of these passages is any other preparation important, such as utterness in consecration, constituting a death to the world, a relinquishment of one's own desires, plans, and ambitions, and an utter dedication of the entire being unto the Lord Jesus Christ and His service alone **for time and eternity?**

A BATTLE ROYAL

Although there is little or no scriptural reference in detail to a period of preparation for the receiving of the Spirit, the Spirit was never given except where an adequate spiritual preparation had actually been made which fully satisfied the heart of God. The fact that the Spirit has come is convincing evidence of this. We do not know how long or short the process, nor its various stages, by which the early disciples reached the condition of total abandonment and commitment. The Scripture is silent on that point. But does anyone doubt that prerequisite conditions satisfactory to the Spirit were met preceding His descent and infilling? **Is it possible that the Spirit comes upon and fills just anyone regardless of his inner moral or spiritual situation?** Will the Spirit fill a vessel that is not empty?

If this question is answered in the negative, then the logical question arises as to what constitutes the conditions prerequisite to faith which bring the outpouring and filling with the Spirit.

It is understood that the only candidates for the baptism or filling with the Spirit are those who have been born again and are walking in all the light they have received (John 14:16, 17). Jesus said that the world, that is, the unregenerate, cannot receive the Spirit. What spiritual preparation is necessary for the believer who is seeking to be filled with the Spirit? In the Pentecostal movement, many seem to receive the Spirit through prayer and the laying on of hands. But others have testified that they received their experience only after a long period of seeking, involving great longing, heart hunger, and sweeping, all-embracing, and unequivocal consecration. In the so-called holiness movement, great stress was laid upon this sort of consecration. Oswald Chambers says that in sanctification, "the regenerated soul deliberately gives up his right to himself to Jesus Christ." He says, "No one enters the experience of entire sanctification without going through a **white funeral** [emphasis added]—the burial of the old life. If there has never been that crisis of death, sanctification is nothing more than a vision." He asks, "Have you come to your last days really? . . . Death means **you** stop being." Here Chambers is thinking of the fallen ego, the self or soulish life, sometimes called the flesh. Sometimes we hear teaching that it is so very easy to be filled with the Spirit. It is said that all we have to do is just believe and receive. Chambers insists, **"There is always a battle royal before sanctification, always something that tugs with resentment against the demands of Jesus Christ."** Jesus said, "If any man will be my disciple, let him deny himself," that is, **his right** to himself. You are not truly consecrated until you are willing to give up your independence and deny your right to your independence.

EVEN THE BEST SELF MUST DIE

In your regeneration you died to sin as an act, that is, you repented of and gave up all willful, premeditated acts of sin. If you did not, your regeneration is in doubt. In sanctification or the filling with the Spirit you die to your own fallen natural life. It is not a question of giving up outbroken sin but of giving up your right to yourself, **Even to your best self. For most of us this is not easy. The old man of the natural life usually dies hard.**

There is an initial act of death in which one gives his consent for all the life of nature and of self to be nailed to the cross. It is an all-inclusive act which embraces all the future for both time and eternity. And, strange as it may seem, this is a progressive thing. As Dr. Watson says, there is a deeper death to self. **At least there are ever-increasing areas of the being that must experience the death of the cross.** And as each new area of the self-life surfaces, the temptation is to refuse the Spirit's challenge to allow it to die, but to come down from the cross.

CHAPTER SEVEN

True Holiness— A Balance Between Experience and Ethics

Therefore, blessed and glorious, real and definite as the crisis of sanctification is, **God is not done with us when we have passed that point.** Sanctification is something more than a blessing, it is a Person, **a Person displacing your own ego.** We do not wish to minimize the experience side of sanctification. I question the genuineness of any experience of sanctification which does not result in a mighty moving of the emotions, called the witness of the Spirit. **But the ethical, not the emotional, content of any religious experience is primary. The real evidence of a sanctified state of grace is not emotional ecstasy or demonstration, but the decentralization of the ego. Self-will is the mother tincture of all sin. Living for self is the essence of all "unholiness." Lucifer became Satan through self-will. The essence of holiness is the "decentralization of the ego," the displacement of self by Christ. You may grow in your ability to demonstrate a certain kind of religious emotional-**

ism without growing in grace. You are growing in grace only when you are growing in meekness, submission, yieldedness, brokenness, and self-lessness.

HOLINESS AND SELF-PROMOTION

Self-promotion is inconsistent with true holiness. Increasing holiness means increasing sensitiveness to sin, increasing tenderness of conscience, increasing repudiation of self-promotion and self-glorification.

When one of our boys was small, he sometimes went visiting for two or three days at a time, and while he was gone, according to the standard of some people, he grew wonderfully in grace. He was very well pleased with himself and if he were called upon to testify, he could probably have said that he was growing in grace. He would return home in that happified state, but it didn't last long. When the discipline of the home, which was absent during his visit, was again brought to bear, he immediately backslid and sometimes there was a stormy and rebellious time. Or did he backslide? I think not. Because of his refusal to come under discipline sweetly when he got back home, his open rebellion against the authority of the home proved that he had not been growing in grace at all. He had actually been growing in ego. He had been spoiled. And when we said to our friends, "Did he act that way for you?" they said, "No-o-o-o, he was just fine for us." I think most of you catch the moral. He only *appeared* to be growing in grace because his will had not been crossed. All of his singing and shouting and demonstration of deep spirituality did not mean a thing except that he was having his own way. And I say again that you are not growing in grace no matter how you appear to be; you are not deeply spiritual no matter how you claim to be, unless you are **growing in meekness, in submission, in yieldedness, and obedience to the discipline of the circumstances and environment in which God has placed you.**

TRUE HOLINESS IS A BALANCE
BETWEEN THEORY AND PRACTICE

Make no mistake about it, **there is no real "decentralization of the ego," and therefore no real depth of holiness while we are seeking to manufacture our own circumstances instead of accepting them as from God.** Refusal to accept the discipline of the circumstances in which God has placed us is evidence of the activity of our own ego. Any real depth of holiness puts an end to this, for it substitutes Christ for our personal self. **If your religious emotion makes you sweeter, kinder, less self-assertive, more meek and submissive, less self-centered and more broken, then it is good.** If it does not, it is probably largely an escape, something by which you avoid facing up to your real self and letting the cross deal with it. In true holiness, there is a balance between experience and ethics.

HOLINESS IS NOT
THEOLOGICAL CORRECTNESS

Another thing behind which much carnal corruption can hide is an exact theology, a theological traditionalism, which some people substitute for the real essence of holiness, **which is meekness, submission, brokenness, defenselessness, and selflessness.** It is possible to be correct, according to the generally accepted teaching of holiness, while tolerating in the life all the earmarks of unbroken self-will. **No one can experience a real crisis of holiness until self-will has been broken.** And no one can keep the experience of the Spirit-filled life who refuses to submit constantly to the breaking work of the cross. No matter how correct your theology, no matter how genuine your initial experience, headiness, rebelliousness, self-assertiveness—all of these will dim and tarnish the fine gold of true holiness. **There is only one place of true holiness and that is on the cross.** In order to experience the crisis of sanctification, you must submit to the actual and practical crucifixion of your old man of sin with Christ. **In order to keep the**

blessing, you must keep your old man of sin on the cross. Whenever you consent that your old life of nature and self shall come down from the cross, the work of sanctification stops instantly in your life. Someone has said, "It is either I or Christ on the cross. Whenever I come down, He goes up again." Right theological views are good, but in all true holiness there must be a balance between theological correctness and actual practice.

TRUE HOLINESS—A BALANCE BETWEEN THE CRISIS AND THE PROCESS

In all true holiness there must be a balance also between the crisis and the process, or **the progressive work of sanctification.** Without the crisis, there can be no process of holiness. Unless the crisis is taught definitely, people will not know how to enter in. But when the crisis becomes a substitute for the process, or the progressive work of the Holy Spirit, the door is opened to a flood of evils and vices which defeat the entire purpose of holiness. **Any teaching which results in a static experience is a curse.** In many instances the teaching of sanctification has been of untold blessing. In others it has been of doubtful value, because it sometimes has failed to inspire spiritual initiative and progress and has induced acquiescence in a static state of grace.

THE DECENTRALIZATION OF SELF

Too long have we tolerated the idea that when one has passed the crisis of sanctification he has arrived, and for him, all or most strenuous endeavor is past. One of the reasons why some people object to the emphasis upon the progressive phase of sanctification is that it gives them absolutely no more excuse for settling down into a static experience than it does the youngest convert. Many people who boast that they came in under the "old constitution" resent having to get out their spiritual picks and shovels and go to digging alongside the new converts in the church. They thought that when they were sanctified or filled with the Spirit, they were through with that. When they discovered that after all they have not arrived, and that in real holiness there is no place to stop, and that as God faces them up with new revelations of their self-life, they must submit to the work of the cross, they sometimes rebel and openly oppose. **But any teaching which makes one comfortable in a static spiritual condition is not, in my judgment, scriptural holiness.**

The heart of true holiness is the ever-increasing decentralization of the ego. That ideal is definitely and clearly set forth in this text, "For me to live is Christ" Philippians 1:21.

THE TRULY HOLY SOUL HAS NO PERSONAL INTERESTS TO SERVE

The soul that is truly delivered from self has no interests of his own to serve. He has no rights nor prerogatives to defend. Such a one is completely delivered from oversensitiveness and readily yields his sensitive nature to the cross. Anything is all right, even imprisonment and death, if it glorifies Christ. It is of little use for us to talk about being ready to die for Christ while we refuse to submit to the cross as it slays our self-life in the endless varieties of daily living. The soul that is truly decentralized accepts all that comes to it of pain or sorrow, of disappointment or slight, of misunderstanding or misconstruction, as an opportunity to die more deeply to the central ego which would contest Christ's sole authority over it. The only question the truly decentralized soul will ask is not "How is this thing going to affect my interests?" but "How is it going to affect Christ's glory?" My feelings, my prerogatives, my comfort, my taste, none of these count. All that matters is that Christ shall be magnified, "whether by life or by death."

CHAPTER EIGHT

The Glorification of Martyrdom

This decentralization of the ego reaches its climax in accepting actual physical death or martyrdom as an opportunity to glorify God. While Paul was doubtless referring to the gain of being with the Lord when he spoke of the gain of death, yet the preceding context reveals that was not the only gain he had in mind, for the whole tenor of the Scripture supports the truth that death may sometimes serve God's ends even better than life. I am not **fully** prepared to serve God, until I am ready, not only to give up my self-life, but also my physical life as well. Most of us think that we must **live** to serve God's purposes. Death in the service of one's country or of humanity is always exalted and glorified. The heroic death of the "Six Hundred" has been immortalized in Tennyson's poem, familiar to every school boy, "The Charge of the Light Brigade." What young heart has not been thrilled by the story of Horatius at the Tiber and the Roman glorification of death for his country. There is the immortal Swiss patriot, Arnold Von Winklried, who gathered in his own bosom the spears of the enemy ranks, opening in an otherwise solid phalanx, a breach into which his countrymen charged and thus made way for liberty and the freedom of his homeland. Coming to more modern times, there is the glorification of death in such poems as "In Flanders' Fields" in the first World War, and finally in the second World War, there is the immortal flag-raising on Iwo Jima. These are only a few of the instances in which men glorify death in the cause of patriotism and humanity.

WE ARE EXPENDABLE

The above is the title of a book written by a war correspondent. It describes the amazing heroism and self-sacrifice of troops trained to spearhead our military operations in the last World War. Graphically the story is told of commando raids, of paratroop invasions, and of spearhead attacks in which a calculated risk of certain death was unhesitatingly accepted with utter calmness, deliberation, and resolution. Before our boys attempted an objective, often they knew they would never return, but they went anyway, because they were expendable.

Think of the quality of courage and devotion to a cause that prompted a gifted and brilliant young poet soldier in the first World War to write these lines:

I have a rendezvous with Death
At some disputed barricade
When Spring comes back with rustling shade
And apple blossoms fill the air.
I have a rendezvous with Death
When Spring brings back blue days and fair.

It may be he shall take my hand,
And lead me into his dark land,
And close my eyes and quench my breath—
It may be I shall pass him still.
I have a rendezvous with Death
On some scarred slope or battered hill,
When Spring comes round again this year
And the first meadow flowers appear.

God knows 'twere better to be deep
Pillowed in silk and scented down
Where love throbs out in blissful sleep,
Pulse nigh to pulse, and breath to breath,
Where hushed awakenings are dear . . .
But I've a rendezvous with Death
At midnight in some flaming town,
When Spring trips north again this year.
And I to my pledged word am true,
I shall not fail that rendezvous.

Alan Seeger, the author, was a young American poet who had made his mark at Harvard. In Paris at the outbreak of the first World War, long before America entered, he joined the French foreign legion. This poem, so full of poignant pathos, reveals the conflicting inner emotions of a young man who loved life, who had a zest for the thrill of spring, who possessed a keen appreciation for the beauty of orchard and meadow in the budding springtime. He was a young man of refined and cultured sensibilities who had known ease and luxury and had felt the thrill of romance and love.

The poem expresses the premonition which Alan Seeger had before "going over the top," but he went anyway, because he was expendable. He fell in action and his lifeless body was later picked up on the field of battle.

What was it that caused this brilliant young man thus to offer himself? It is what we call patriotism. It was the same spirit which actuated the gallant Six Hundred immortalized in Tennyson's "Charge of the Light Brigade." Although they knew the command to charge was a blunder, although they knew it was certain death, yet

Theirs not to make reply,
Theirs not to reason why,
Theirs but to do and die,

because they were expendable.

PATRIOTS ARE EXPENDABLE, MANY CHRISTIANS ARE NOT

During the last war, the Rev. E. A. Burroughs referred to "patriotism" as a religion which does what Christianity talks about, a religion which is "more Christian than Christianity" itself as the twentieth century has come to regard it. How could a man make such a statement? What could be its basis? Simply this, that the central principle of Christianity is self-sacrifice, expendability.

And the world sees in the self-immolation, the self-forgetfulness, the surrender even unto death on the part of soldiers and patriots, a more perfect example of the central principle of Christianity than they see, with few exceptions, in the professed followers of Christ. In other words, patriots have shown more willingness to die for love of country than many of us show to die for Christ. Patriots are expendable. Few Christians are. Nevertheless, since the cross, the death to love of ease, love of family, love of life itself, is the central principle of Christianity. Since the world sees this principle operating more powerfully in patriots than in many professed Christians and in ordinary twentieth-century Christianity, it regards patriotism as "more Christian than Christianity." Patriots demonstrate more heroically the Christian principle of "death to self" than do most of us. We have surrendered the central principle of Christianity to patriots. That is why the nation deifies its war heroes, because men instinctively recognize the divine quality of self-sacrifice, of "not loving one's life unto death," of being expendable. The world still recognizes and admires the cross principle, the example of self-sacrifice, wherever they see it in action.

COMMUNISTS ARE EXPENDABLE, MANY CHRISTIANS ARE NOT

But we have not only surrendered this world-moving principle to patriotism, we have surrendered it to Communism. Maurice Thorez, a former leader of the Communist party in France, during a five-hour speech to a Communist rally in Paris said that he was shocked at the "unbelievable passiveness" of many Communist leaders and then made this shocking statement: "The blood of the martyrs brings the quickest harvest." Fancy a Communist using the principle of the cross to promote Communism. Communists are expendable. By the use of the central principle of Christianity, Communism threatens to engulf the world. We, the followers of the Lord Jesus

Christ, preach the cross, but patriots and Communists practice it. And in that particular respect they may be regarded as more Christian than many of us. The Church can save itself only as it works out this principle of the Cross more fully than its antagonists do.

In Los Angeles sometime ago, a personal worker is reported to have spoken to a man on the street about his spiritual need. That man turned on him and said, "I am a Communist. As a Communist, I am not my own. I am prepared to sacrifice my job, my home, my wife, my family, and even my very life, if I am called upon to do so. I am expendable." Here was a man who, for the sake of an atheistic political ideology, was accepting the principle of the cross and getting absolutely nothing for it except the chance to die, while millions of professing Christians evade the cross principle. Patriots and Communists, for their less worthy and low ends, gladly embrace the principle of the cross, while the Church at large seeks to shun it.

Let me remind you of the words of Marshall Foch: "Battles are won by teaching soldiers how to die, not how to avoid dying." And the battles of the cross are won in no other way. Unless today we can produce a type of discipline comparable at least to that of the patriot or the Communist, are we worthy to survive?

Preparing to cross the Alps, Napoleon addressed his soldiers: "You have gained battles without cannon, passed rivers without bridges, performed forced marches without shoes, bivouacked without strong liquors and often without bread. Thanks for your perseverance! But soldiers, you have done nothing—for there remains much to do!" So spoke Napoleon to his men, and they rallied to him as leader. But a greater than Napoleon appeals today.

Garibaldi, the liberator of Italy, said: "I am going out from Rome. I offer neither pay, nor quarters, nor provisions; I offer hunger, thirst, forced marches, battles, death. Let him who loves his country in his heart and not with his lips only, follow me." But a greater than Garibaldi speaks today.

CHRISTIANITY'S LOST NOTE OF HEROISM

What has become of the note of heroism in modern Christianity? While the world glorifies death for patriotic or humanitarian purposes, while the world immortalizes as heroes many who volunteer for death, the Church sits in criticism upon those who demonstrate a like devotion to Christ and cynically says with Judas, "To what purpose is this waste?" The Apostle distinctly says that "to die is gain." Was Stephen's death a gain? As someone has pointed out, Stephen died, and through his death, Christ got His Great Apostle. Stephen never could have done what the Apostle Paul did. A hundred or even a thousand Stephens probably could not have accomplished what God did through Paul. But Stephen could die and give God a chance to get His Great Apostle. Every student of Bible history knows that only one of the Apostles died a natural death—that "the blood of the martyrs is the seed of the church."

WAS CHRIST'S DEATH A WASTE?

The great example of the gain of death is the death of our Lord Jesus Christ. All of the arguments in favor of self-preservation could have been advanced in favor of Christ's escape from death. To His disciples and friends it doubtless seemed a senseless waste of precious life when Jesus died so young and in such shame. No doubt, when He was lying in the grave, His friends spoke together of what a great loss to the world His death was. Perhaps they thought He had been imprudent and reckless—almost throwing away His life. Peter may have talked about how he had tried to keep Him from going up to Jerusalem to meet death. It seemed to them all perhaps that His death was a sad loss to the world. According to natural analogy, had Jesus saved His life from the cross, He might have lived to a ripe old age, making all His years as beautiful as the three or four years of His ministry. **But there would have been no cross lifted up to draw all men by its wondrous power of love.**

There would have been no fountain opened to which Earth's penitent millions could come with their polluted lives to find cleansing. There would have been no atonement for human guilt, no tasting of death for every man, no sacrifice for the sin of the world. **There would have been no broken grave with its victory over death, and eternal life for all who believe.** Christ lost His life, but it became the seed of the world's hope and joy. Truly, in His case, death was gain.

THE LAW OF LIFE

Calvary is God's sublime master model for us all. It carries the law of life for all of us. "To die is gain." "He that loveth his life shall lose it; and he that hateth his life in this world shall keep it unto life eternal" John 12:25.

DEATH IN LIFE OR LIFE THROUGH DEATH

The world has glorified sacrificial death. Dare we do any less? In the annals of human history, in poetry and art, to die for home and country is to cover oneself with glory. In World War II in Germany, to die for Hitler was to cover oneself with glory. In Japan, to die for the Emperor was to cover oneself with glory. Today in Russia, to die for Mother Russia is to cover oneself with glory. **Is Christ less worthy than Hitler? Is Christ less worthy than the Japanese Emperor? Is Christ less worthy than Mother Russia, or America the beautiful? Is the Kingdom of God less worthy than human thrones and kingdoms?**

Norman Grubb tells us that in the early centuries of the Church, when Christians faced the constant threat of martyrdom, the elders of the Church were asked this question before hands of consecration were laid on them: "Art thou then able to drink of the cup which I am about to drink or be baptized with the baptism with which I am about to be baptized?" To which they answered, "I take on myself scourgings, imprisonment, tortures, reproaches, crosses, blows, tribulation, and all the temptations of the world which our Lord, and Intercessor, and the Universal, and Apostolic Holy Church took upon themselves."

Whoever will choose the same destiny as Christ, must take the same road He took. **It is a universal eternal law. It is either life through death or death in life. Self-seeking is self-destruction.** This has been forever verified as the law of the universe in Philippians 2:6-11. "Who, being in the form of God, thought it not robbery to be equal with God: but made himself of no reputation, and took upon him the form of a servant, and was made in the likeness of men: and, being found in fashion as a man, he humbled himself, and became obedient unto death, even the death of the cross. Wherefore God also hath highly exalted him, and given him a name which is above every name: that at the name of Jesus every knee should bow, of things in heaven, and things in earth, and things under the earth; and that every tongue should confess that Jesus Christ is Lord, to the glory of God the Father." Hallelujah!

Verily, the cross is the throne of the universe.

PART II

"As Dying, and, Behold, We Live"
A New Year's Message

CHAPTER NINE
Looking at the Need

"Not as though I had already attained ..." Philippians 3:12.

One of the greatest enemies of progress is self-complacency, satisfaction with goals already reached, with achievements already attained. One of the things which I believe grieves the heart of God almost more than anything is the ease with which we are satisfied in spiritual things. One of the greatest hindrances to the advancement of the Kingdom of God is the tendency to accept our present spiritual attainments as the **ultimate** and to cease further spiritual exploration. It is not good always to be tinkering with ourselves. It is not good to be an introvert, always looking within. But it is worse to be so self-satisfied that we never take an inventory, or to be afraid to look inside.

THE NECESSITY OF FIRM PURPOSE

Progress and growth cease when we lose the spirit of adventure. The ideal Christian life is one of insatiable thirst, never pausing in any arbor of spiritual content but ever wooed by visions of new heights of spiritual attainment. One of the things which must grieve the heart of God is the smallness of the obstacles which we allow to hinder us or turn us aside from the path of high resolve. We start out into a new year, or upon a new course of spiritual endeavor, full of energy and enthusiasm. But it takes a very little to slow us down and sometimes even to turn us back from our new adventure. As soon as we discover that the attainment of new spiritual heights demands energy, firm resolution, over-coming of obstacles, the loss of ease and comfort, the denying of the flesh, we are too often ready to give up the task. On the tomb of an Alpine guide is this inscription, "He died climbing," I am very conscious of my lack of the gentler graces of the Spirit and am praying that God may help me to be less stern in standing for my convictions, in my striving for spiritual achievement, and in my efforts to challenge others. But I pray even more that when I lay my armor down, it may truly be said of me, "He died climbing."

THE PRICE OF SPIRITUAL PROGRESS

How few of us are willing to pay the price for spiritual progress. **"There can be no spiritual progress except through the death of self. Every step on the pathway of spiritual progress will be marked by the bloody footprints of wounded self-love"** (Maclaren). All along the course of spiritual advancement you will have to set up altars upon which even the **legitimate** self-life will have to be sacrificed. And not very many of us are willing to take this way. Whenever anything threatens pain or inconvenience to the self-life, many of us draw back and seek an easier way. We will avoid anything that brings discomfort, that does not please the flesh. One manifestation of this tendency seen all around us is an army of believers who run from one church to another, from one congregation to another, not because they are seeking more of God, but because they are seeking to evade death to the self-life. Such people may indeed spend much of their lives trying to find a place to worship where their spiritual ego will be exalted and inflated, where they are more culturally comfortable and find more emotional pleasure, but they do so at the cost of possible spiritual progress. **They often mistake shallow emotionalism for deep spirituality** and delude themselves into thinking **that enjoyment in worship is its primary purpose.** Spiritual progress is the result, not of nurturing the natural self-life, or even the religious self-life, but of *yielding it to the cross*.

THE APOSTLE'S CHALLENGE

How refreshing it is to hear the great Apostle confessing his lack, acknowledging his need, and admitting his shortcoming. "Not as though I had already attained, neither were already perfect," that is, perfect in the sense of resurrection perfection. If he had stopped there, there would have been no challenge. But he did not stop there. "But this one thing I do." And what was that toward which all of Paul's energies were bent? It was spiritual progress. "Forgetting those things which are behind, and reaching forth unto those things which are before, I press toward the mark for the prize of the high calling of God in Christ Jesus." Here is set forth the method of progress.

UNBROKEN MEN OF LITTLE USE

According to our Lord's teaching, we can make the most out of life by losing it. He says that the losing of life for His sake is saving it. There is a lower self that must be trampled down. **But there is also a higher self that must be slain. The alabaster vase, beautiful as it is, must be broken, that the ointment may flow forth and its fragrance fill the house. The grapes must be crushed before there can be wine to drink. The wheat must be bruised before it can become bread to feed the hungry.** "Bread corn is bruised" Isaiah 28:28.

It is so in life. **"Whole, unbruised, unbroken men are of but little use to God"** (J. R. Miller). Until we cease to live for self, we have not begun to live at all. Only as the law of self-sacrifice becomes a heart principle can any life become the blessing to the world it was intended to be. In one of his little books J. R. Miller illustrates this principle as follows:

A great oak stands in the forest. It is beautiful in its majesty; it is ornamental; it casts a pleasant shade. Under its branches the children play; among its boughs the birds sing. One day the woodman comes with his axe, and the tree quivers in all its branches under his sturdy blows. "I am being destroyed," it cries. So it seems, as the great tree crashes down to the ground. And the children are sad because they can play no more beneath the broad branches; the birds grieve because they can no more nest and sing amid the summer foliage.

WE DIE TO LIVE

But let us follow the tree's history. It is cut into boards, and built into a beautiful cottage, where human hearts find their happy nest. Or it is used in making a great organ which leads the worship of a congregation. The losing of its life was the saving of it. It dies that it might become deeply, truly useful.

The plates, cups, dishes, and vases which we use in our homes and on our tables once lay as common clay in the earth, quiet and restful, but in no way doing good, serving man. Then came men with picks, and the clay was rudely torn out and plunged into a mortar and beaten and ground in a mill, then pressed and put into a furnace, and burned and burned, at last coming forth in beauty and beginning its history of usefulness. It was apparently destroyed that it might begin to be of service.

NO LIFE EXCEPT BY DEATH

A great church-building is going up, and the stones that are being laid on the walls are brought out of the dark quarry for this purpose. We can imagine them complaining, groaning, and repining, as the quarry-men's drills and hammers struck them. They supposed they were being destroyed as they were torn out from the bed of rock where they had lain undisturbed for ages, and were cut into blocks, and lifted out, and then chiselled and dressed into form. But they were being destroyed only that they might become useful. They become part of a new sanctuary in which God is to be worshipped, where the Gospel will be preached, where penitent sinners will find the Christ-Savior, where sorrowing ones will be comforted. Surely it was better that these stones should be torn out, even amid agony, and built into the wall of the church, than that they should have lain ages more, undisturbed in the dark quarry. They were saved from uselessness by being destroyed.

There are many illustrations of the principle that we must die in order to be useful, to be truly a blessing. The seed must die to bear fruit. The mother must enter the jaws of death in order to give birth.

There is no gain but by a loss;
You cannot save but by a cross.
The corn of wheat to multiply,
Must fall into the ground and die.
Wherever you ripe fields behold,
Waving to God their sheaves of gold,
Be sure some corn of wheat has died,
Some soul has there been crucified,
Someone has wrestled, wept, and prayed,
And fought hell's legions undismayed.

Life everywhere replaces death,
In earth and sea and sky;
And that the rose may breathe its breath,
Some living thing must die.

But all through life I see a cross,
Where sons of God yield up their breath;
There is no gain except by loss,
There is no life except by death.
And no full vision except by Faith,
Nor glory but by wearing shame,

Nor justice but by taking blame;
And that Eternal Passion saith,
"Be emptied of glory and right and name."

THE CORN OF WHEAT

Some have said that our son Paul Rollin's life was wasted when he gave it to missions, and then died on the field just a few weeks after arriving. Although he was not permitted to minister, large numbers of young people arose to be trained for the harvest field where he hoped to reap and have picked up the sickle which he laid down. The "corn of wheat" that fell in Mexico has been multiplied many times and still the work goes on. In 1948 a new school to reach a new tribe was opened in his memory. Had Paul Rollin lived many years at home it is doubtful if he could have done the work which he did in a few short weeks which ended in his death. And he is only one of many like examples which illustrate the truth that "except a corn of wheat fall into the ground and die, it abideth alone."

THE BROKEN ALABASTER BOX

Mary's ointment was "wasted" when she broke her vase and poured it on the Lord. The natural man would say "yes," along with the disciples. Yes; but suppose she had left it in the unbroken vase? Would there have been any mention of it? Would her deed of careful keeping have been told all over the world? She broke the vase and poured the ointment forth, lost it, sacrificed it, and now the perfume incense has drifted into every home where this message has been heard. We may keep our life if we will, carefully preserving it from waste, but we shall have no reward. But if we empty it out in loving service, we shall make it a lasting blessing to the world, and we shall be remembered forever. **The altar of sacrifice stands in the foreground of every life and cannot be bypassed except at the cost of all that is noblest and best. We cannot save ourselves and save others. We must burn in order to give out light.**

CHAPTER TEN

Wisdom of Forgetting

Another step in Paul's process of development was death to the past. "Forgetting those things which are behind." It has been said that it takes courage and resolution to continue ever moving away from the past. We would like to keep the things we have learned to love, and we do not want to move away from them. It is difficult for some people to leave their sorrows behind, to come out of the shadows of their griefs. It is difficult to come away from the graves where we have buried our heart treasures.

THE PURPOSE OF GRIEF

But this is not God's will for us. Of course grief, if it is submissive grief, is not wrong. We cannot but miss sweet companionships. Life can doubtless never be the same again for some who are sorrowing. But the losses and griefs of life have been intended to leave behind a richness of character and blessing which will make eternity richer. Sooner or later, sorrow comes to every home. No condition of wealth or culture or even of religion can exclude it. When two young people come from the marriage altar and set up their new home, it seems to them their joy can never be disturbed, that grief can never reach their hearts in that charmed spot. For a few years, perhaps, their fond dream remains unbroken. The flowers bloom in still softer hues and richer fragrance; the music continues light and joyous with no minor chords. The circle is unbroken; child-lives grow up in the tender atmosphere, blessing the home with their love and lovableness; the household life flows on softly and smoothly like a river, gathering in breadth and depth as it flows. In other homes, all about, there are sorrows, bereavements, or worse. But amid the desolations of other homes, this one remains untouched, like an oasis on the desert.

But not forever. There comes a day when the sable-clad messenger of sorrow stands at the door and lays his withering hand on some sweet flower. Perhaps I am now speaking to one such home where grief has entered for the first time in recent months.

THE DANGER OF GRIEF

The first experience of grief is very sore. Its sadness and strangeness add to its terribleness. What seemed so impossible yesterday has become a fearful reality today. The dear one we had held so securely, we thought, is gone now. It seems to us that we can never be comforted, that we can never live without the one who filled such a large place in our life. The time of the first sorrow is to every life a most critical point. Many persons find in grief an enemy only, to whom they refuse to be reconciled. Sorrow may be either a blessing or a curse. Someone has said, "Don't waste your sorrows." Whether sorrow will be a blessing or a curse depends upon the relation of the sufferer to Christ. The same fire that melts the wax, hardens the clay. Sorrow is a fire which in God's hand is designed to melt and purify the lives of His people, but which, if resisted and unaccepted, produces desolation. In a Christian life or a Christian home, sorrow should always leave a benediction. It should be received as God's messenger, and when it is, it will leave a blessing of peace and will make the home sweeter, more tender, and more heavenly. It has been said that no home ever attains its highest blessedness and joy, and its fullest richness of life, until in some way sorrow enters its door. "Even the home love, like certain autumn fruits, does not ripen into its sweetest tenderness until the frosts of trial have touched it."

THE BLESSING OF SORROW

Many of the world's best things have been born of affliction. The sweetest songs that have ever been sung have come out of the fire. The good things we inherit from the past are the purchase of suffering and sacrifice. Our redemption comes through Gethsemane and Calvary. We get Heaven through Christ's tears and blood. Whatever is richest and best in any life has been forged in fire. Our love for one another may be strong and true, but it never reaches its holiest and fullest expression until pain has touched our hearts. Even the love of a mother never reaches its full measure of strength until the child suffers or is in danger. The same is true of all the home loves. The household that has endured sorrow in the true spirit of submission and faith, emerges from it with purer, more tender affection, with less of selfishness, fleshliness and earthiness. When husband and wife stand together beside their dead child, they are drawn closer together than ever before. Children that remain gain a new preciousness. Brothers and sisters grow more thoughtful when the home circle has been broken. A vacant chair in a Christian home has a wondrous power to soften and refine the affections and feelings. The cloud of grief that hangs over a home is rich with blessings and is ready to break upon the sufferers' heads. (Adapted from J. R. Miller)

DON'T WASTE YOUR SORROWS
How may we be sure of receiving the blessings of sorrow? First, we must recognize it as a messenger from God. We must accept it as coming from Him, that is, with His permission. All sorrow originates with sin or Satan, but all is under God's control. We must listen for the message in spite of the loss and pain. It may take us a good while to hear it. The first experience of sorrow may leave us so stunned and blinded that we seem to be in total darkness. It may be a long time before our vision will be cleared. **All of the promises that once meant so much to us may seem to be utterly meaningless now. We will be tempted to doubt all those things we once most surely believed.** But God is near, even when we cannot see Him. And as we refuse the temptation to charge God foolishly, as we listen for His voice, as

we gradually yield our rebellion and accept our sorrow as from Him, we will discover it has some mission to perform, some gift from heaven, some golden fruit. **We will see that some bit of gold in us has been set free from its dross by this fire. Don't be discouraged if it takes some time to get this blessing. Wait; wait! It will come.**

But we must remember that these things are true only in lives and homes where Christ dwells. A Christless home receives none of these treasures of sorrow. Those who shut their doors on Christ shut out all blessedness, and when the lamps of earthly joy go out, they are left in utter darkness.

> *Alas for him who never sees*
> *The stars shine through his cypress trees;*
> *Who hopeless lays his dead away,*
> *Nor looks to see the light of day,*
> *Across the mossy marbles play.*
>
> John Greenleaf Whittier

FORGETTING OUR MISTAKES

Some of us find it difficult not only to forget our sorrows, but to forget our mistakes. Doubtless, the past year has had its number of mistakes. Probably they hang threateningly over our memories and exert a disheartening influence over us as we face the future. If we are not careful, the mistakes of the past can hang like chains about us, effectively hindering our progress. We are tempted to feel that we can never succeed because we have failed in the past.

MISTAKES MAY BECOME A BLESSING

It may surprise us to know that past mistakes need not only be no hindrance, but may actually be a blessing. **We actually grow by making mistakes.** Before the artist can put a masterpiece on canvas, he must experience many failures due to mistakes. Before the musician is able to thrill an audience with his talent, he must spend years making mistakes and correcting them. In every department of life there are years and years with little but mistakes, immaturities, blunders, while men and women are preparing for beautiful living and noble work.

GOD CAN OVERRULE

Comfort for those of us whose past lies heavily upon us because of mistakes, should be found in Jeremiah's visit to the potter, and God's message about the potter and his work. In Jeremiah 18:4 we read, "And the vessel that he made of clay was marred in the hands of the potter." That is not a bright picture. Doubtless, many of us can see our own faces in this mirror. We have failed God. We have not lived up to our best because of our own insensitivity and self-will; we have been vessels marred in the hands of the potter, and now we are living under the tyranny of a regret-filled past which enervates and robs us of enterprise.

Some of our preaching presents God in such an inflexible mood as to discourage a frank confession of failure and a second effort at renewal. But one of the clearest revelations of the Word of God, and particularly of this incident in question, is the truth that declares God's willingness to restore to men the mercies which they have forfeited; that He renews the grace they have misused; that every year and even every day may be one of new beginning. "And the vessel that he made of clay was marred in the hands of the potter." Was the potter baffled thereby? Did he give up his purpose? Did he throw aside the clay after one failure? "So he made it again, another vessel."

IF AT FIRST YOU DON'T SUCCEED

I have been under the impression for years that the second vessel which the potter made was less beautiful and useful than the one he would have made if it had not been marred. But I have been told recently by one who works in clay that the second vessel made out of a failure may be even better than the one originally attempted. I have been told that the additional working of the clay renders it more pliable and yielding and that the second vessel may be even more honorable than the first. And God said to Jeremiah, as He watched the potter refashion another vessel out of the clay, "O house of Israel, cannot I do with you as this potter?" Jeremiah 18:6. If he can make another and perhaps even a better vessel from the first abortive attempt, cannot God take a marred life and make it into a thing of beauty and joy? "Behold, as clay in the potter's hand, so are ye in mine hand, O house of Israel" Jeremiah 18:6. To all who have thought that by your failures you have forfeited a second opportunity, these words are spoken: "I will restore to you the years that the locust hath eaten, the cankerworm, and the caterpillar, and the palmer-worm" Joel 2:25.

Think of all of the biblical characters who failed and were later restored. There is Jacob, who after his deception (Genesis 27) is visited by God with a vision of the ladder and of the angels and of the throne of God, and was given the assurance that God had not given him up (Genesis 28). There is Moses, who after his miserable failure early in life, is carefully tutored by God for forty years at the backside of the desert and then recommissioned for his original task (Exodus 3). There is David, who after his most heinous crime is trusted to start afresh (2 Samuel 12; Psalm 51). Remember Jonah, who turned his back upon his mission, but received the Word of God the second time and was sent again to take up the task he had deserted (Jonah 3). Consider Peter, who denied Jesus three times, with cursing and swearing, and who yet was the subject of a special invitation to rejoin his old fellowship (Mark 16:7). Think of Thomas, who failed so miserably in his faith and yet was reinvested with his old office (John 20:27). And finally, look at John Mark, who went to pieces in the beginning, but was renewed and restored and, in the end, made good (2 Timothy 4:11). All of these examples encourage us to believe that the past, whatever its delinquencies, need not tyrannize our lives; that failure, however inexcusable, need not be a permanent handicap; and that God's grace is not exhausted by His first gifts. These examples teach us that a new life may be organized out of the old.

AS SEEMED GOOD TO THE POTTER

"So he made it again another vessel" Jeremiah 18:4. This is a message to those who have somehow ceased to try because they once have failed. Some failure has brought them to the dust in humiliation and shame. The nerve of all their effort has been cut or paralyzed, and it seems hardly worthwhile to try again. But the Divine Potter, like Jeremiah's potter, is not so easily discouraged. "He will not fail nor be discouraged." "So He made it again another vessel." And the second effort evidently resulted in a vessel that pleased the potter. "As seemed good to the potter to make it." Moffatt translates this "to please himself till he was satisfied." It is true that all sin, error, or mistakes must be considered a liability. And yet, such is the grace of God that when they are truly repented of, He may overrule them all for His glory. And the second vessel which the potter made seemed good to the potter.

THE PATHWAY OF REPENTANCE

It must not be overlooked, however, that while potter's clay is inert and insensate, human clay is not. In the case of a human life, the ability of the Divine Potter to remake the human vessel and to organize victory out of defeat, depends upon, first of all, **a clear knowledge of the mistake, then a clear acknowledging of it**, that is, a confession, and finally a real repentance and correcting of it. For God said to Jeremiah, "O house of Israel, cannot I do with you as this potter? ... At what instant I shall speak concerning a nation, and concerning a kingdom, to pluck up, and to pull down, and to destroy it; if that nation ... turn from their evil, I will repent of the evil that I thought to do unto them" Jeremiah 18:6-8. This principle is just as valid in individual life. The moment we have realized a mistake and truly repent and correct it and make adjustment, that moment God reverses the trend of evil that would follow. The reversal of the evil trend is instantaneous. "At what instant," God says. No matter what the mistake or failure may be, the moment you turn to God in penitence, correction, and adjustment, that moment things will begin to change. **But the mistake must be recognized in particular.** It is not enough to acknowledge mistakes in general. **We must single out and define the mistake in so many words. We must face up on specific propositions. We must have a clear definition of our mistake in order to correct it and to get God's forgiveness.** And the moment the correction is made, we must do as Paul did; we must place the whole thing in God's hands and accept the forgiveness which He gives. From then on it is no more of our business, and we should forget it. When God forgives us, we must forgive ourselves. This is the pathway to victory over past mistakes and failures. "Forgetting those things which are behind" Philippians 3:13.

FORGETTING OUR HURTS

Another thing we should forget are the hurts we have received in the past. All of us have them. **We cherish them at our own peril.** We have all known of individuals who have almost lost a hand or an arm because of a tiny splinter which somehow got into the finger and was permitted to stay there until blood poisoning set in. That is the way with little hurts. When they are kept in memory, they fester and sometimes produce fatal results. **Some of us have SUFFERED GREAT WRONGS IN THE PAST.** Perhaps the hopes and efforts and dreams of a lifetime have been completely dashed by the perfidy of a trusted friend. Maybe someone whom you have befriended has betrayed you and has treacherously turned to become your enemy. Maybe someone you trusted has proved false and has sought to destroy you. Well, if you cherish such hurts and harbor resentment in your heart, you will indeed suffer harm. We need often to be reminded that nothing that anyone else can do to us can harm us unless it causes us to do wrong, unless we permit a wrong attitude or reaction. In the last analysis, no one in all the world can really harm us but ourselves. Only our reaction can really injure us. The hurts that have come to us in the past year, if forgiven and forgotten, can become stepping-stones to greatness of character, by teaching us a new dimension of agape love, and in the end can be the means of great spiritual growth and blessing by enhancing our eternal rank. Since it is not the wrong which others do to us which injures us, but only our wrong reaction and attitude, it is, therefore, better to suffer wrong than to do wrong.

FORGETTING PAST ATTAINMENTS

We should also forget our past attainments, our success and achievements. "We should never regard any noble deed of ours as our best. We should never look back for the climax of our attainment or achievement" (J. R. Miller). However noble and useful your past year was, however much you did for Christ and your fellowmen, it should never be regarded as the *Ne plus ultra* beyond which we cannot reach. All of our past should be dwarfed by our vision of the future. "We are to win high altitudes in life by leaving and forgetting the things that are behind."

CHAPTER ELEVEN

The Slowness of the Process

We come now to the forward look. "Reaching forth unto those things that are before." Moffat translates it, "Straining to what lies before me." I sense in this phraseology the spirit of holy impatience. One of the most difficult experiences of a high soul, of a soul with a sublime spiritual urge, is the apparent slowness of his spiritual growth, the slowness of God's making of him. And yet we must remember that in one sense even God has to have time in order to make a saint, just as He takes time to make an oak tree. It is true that incipient sainthood is the work of an instant. The moment that a child of God is born again **that moment all the possibilities of sainthood are born in him.** But the developing and realizing of those potentialities is often the work of years and it is very easy to become impatient with God over the slowness of the process. Even when we are straining to the things that are before us, beckoning us on to the sublime heights of Christian character, the process of realization is often slow. It has been well said that **"God does not make us all at once. The process is a long one, running through all the years of our life. God begins making us when we are born and His work goes on continuously all our days. There is never an hour when some new touch is not given to our life, some new line marked out in our character"** (J. R. Miller). A thousand agencies and influences have part in this work: mother, father, the home, the school, the playground, the church, books, companions, friends and friendships, joys and sorrows, successes, failures, health, sickness, roses, briars—all life's circumstances and events. These things all work upon us, **yet not blindly, not without guidance.** God is always on the field and He works in and through all experiences, unless we drive Him out of our life.

IT IS GOD WHO FASHIONS US

If this is true, although we see only the circumstances, **it is really God who makes us.** To be sure, we cannot see His hand for it is hidden behind the circumstances, **but it is really His hand that is shaping us.** There is no period in all the years when we can say that God has finished making us.

A young woman who lost her two babies, both in one day, became rebellious, and, as a result of her grieving, became an invalid. One day she said to her aunt, who was older and much wiser in spiritual things, "I wonder why God made me. I don't know what was the use of making me." And her aunt replied, "Perhaps not much yet, but He hasn't done with you yet. He is making you now, and you don't like it."

It might help some of us to remember that God isn't through with us yet. **He is still making us.** We might not be so impatient with ourselves and God if we always kept in mind that we are only in the process of being made. It might help us to understand better the reasons for the hard or painful experiences that come to us. **God is at work on us with mallet and chisel like a master sculptor working on a piece of stone.**

NOTHING ACCIDENTAL

At present we are not what we should be, neither are we what we shall be. **But God does not work without a pattern or a design. He knows what He is doing regardless of our blindness. There is nothing accidental about the providences that come into our lives.** There is a hand that is guiding and controlling these situations and there is a purpose running through all the events and circumstances. This purpose may not be evident to us, but there is an eye that always watches the pattern. It is God who fashions us.

> Tis the Master who holds the mallet,
>   And day by day
> He is chipping whatever environs
>   The form away,
> Which, under His skillful cutting,
>   He means shall be
> Wrought silently out of beauty
>   Of such degree
> Of faultless and full perfection,
>   That angel eyes

Shall look on the finished labor
  With new surprise,
That even His boundless patience
  Could grave His own
Features upon such fractured
  And stubborn stone.

GOD IS NOT DONE WITH US YET

It has been well said that we should never pass judgment upon unfinished work of any kind. An unripe apple is not fit to eat, but we should not, therefore, condemn it. It is not yet ready for eating, because God is not done making it. Its unripeness is the precise condition which belongs to it at its present stage. It is a phase of its career and good in its place. We have no right to judge a work until it is finished. No artist will submit his picture for inspection while it is in an incomplete state. Neither is it just and right for us to form opinions upon God's providences until their purpose is complete.

We should apply this rule to all that God is doing in us and with us. We should never mistake the process for the final result. **God has not finished with us yet.** Not much that is worthy and beautiful may have come to perfection in us yet. We continue to make blunders and mistakes. We never seem to get our lessons all learned. Just when we think we have learned them, we discover our error in an attempt to practice them. We never seem to get them fully wrought out in life. But we must remember that we are only learners, scholars at school. From God's angle we are only children, not men. **The picture is not painted yet. The fruit is not ripe yet. But some day the work will be complete and we shall be presented "faultless before the presence of his glory with exceeding joy" Jude 24. We must wait until the last chapter of life is written before we say that God is not good or kind.**

I will not doubt, though all my ships at sea
  Come drifting home with broken masts and sails;

I will believe the Hand which never fails,
  From seeming evil worketh good for me.
And though I weep because those sails are tattered,
  Still will I cry, while my best hopes lie
  shattered.
    "I trust in Thee."
I will not doubt, though all my prayers return
  Unanswered from the still, white realm above;
  I will believe it is an all-wise love
Which has refused these things for which I yearn;
  And though at times I cannot keep from grieving,
  Yet the pure ardor of my fixed believing
    Undimmed shall burn.
I will not doubt, though sorrows fall like rain,
  And troubles swarm like bees about a hive.
  I will believe the heights for which I strive
Are only reached by anguish and by pain;
  And though I groan and writhe beneath my crosses,
  I yet shall see through my severest losses
    The greater gain.
I will not doubt. Well anchored is this faith,
Like some staunch ship, my soul braves every gale;
  So strong its courage that it will not quail
To breast the mighty unknown sea of death.
  Oh, may I cry, though body parts with spirit,
"I do not doubt," so listening worlds may hear it.
  With my last breath.

THIS IS NOT THE DEVIL'S WORLD

Believing this, we shall face the worst that life can bring without doubting the outcome of any experience or combination of experiences, as long as we are trusting Him and doing His will. **This is not a world of chance— there is no chance anywhere. This is not the devil's world. "The Lord reigneth"** Psalm 96:10. The divine hand is active in all the affairs of earth. If we are loyal and faithful to Him in all experiences, we shall find in the end that in nothing has our Master erred, for He doeth all things well.

"He [Jesus] regulates the universe by the mighty power of His command" Hebrews 1:3 (TLB).

CHAPTER TWELVE

Concentration

We should not forget that while a saint is not made in a day, **neither is a saint made in his sleep.** Therefore, if we are to realize our visions and reach our goals, we, like Paul, must "strain to what lies before." That is, all the power of our being must be concentrated on this business of spiritual growth. Before us, as we face the future, we have caught a glimpse of ideal spiritual beauty and we long to reach it. If we are not careful, we are in danger of missing the best way of realizing our ideals, of working out our visions. We are in danger of thinking that high goals are going to be reached by emotional cataclysm, by ecstatic experiences. In moments of great inspiration, a holy fervor has been kindled and we think we are ready for great heroisms, for large tasks, for splendid self-denials. **But the test of life to which most of us are called during the week will not be in conspicuous things which people will talk about, but in the common, humdrum things of daily life.** And because of this, we are in danger of missing the opportunity to work out our visions in a practical way.

ENVY OF ANGELS

One of Murillo's pictures shows the interior of a kitchen. Instead, however, of mortals in working dress, we see angels in white garments at the lowly work. One is putting the kettle on the fire, another is lifting a pail of water, another is setting the table. Then there is a little cherub also offering his assistance. The lesson is that the most lowly tasks which we are called upon to do, **if done from the right motive,** are really so heavenly in character that angels could fittingly and would gladly do them. But because of our uncrucified ego we are in danger of overlooking the sacredness of common tasks, and while we are waiting for some conspicuous task in which to realize our ideals, our real opportunity passes unimproved. It might surprise us to know how glad angels would be to step into our shoes and take up our lowly tasks. Some mother, who frets over the fact that she is tied down by the responsibility of rearing a family, while her neighbor is free to mingle in society, may some day make the startling discovery that she was the envy of angels. "And whosoever shall exalt himself shall be abased; and he that shall humble himself shall be exalted" Matthew 23:12 (New Scofield).

LOWLY TASKS—HEAVENLY GRACE

Lowly tasks offer just as great an opportunity to develop heavenly graces as more conspicuous ones. More heavenly grace is required oftentimes for common tasks than for ostensibly great things. Sometimes we think we could go to a martyr's death for Christ, when we are unwilling to live a martyr's life for Him. The chances are that our glowing heavenly visions, born in moments of high resolve, will have to be tested and worked out in the endless varieties of lowly circumstances. These thoughts have been expressed by an unknown writer in the following lines:

"I have seen the vision of thee, O Christ!
  Now what wilt thou have me to do?
For the hardest work in all the world
  I offer Thee service true."

"Go back, my child, to thy little cares;
  Thou hast not known them very long.
Bear for me yet a little while
  Thy feeling of bitter wrong."

"Lord Christ, I am ready for martyrdom
  For banishment, death or pain."
"Patiently still thine heartache hide;
  Sing at thy task again."

"I am strong and eager and loving, Lord;
  I have courage rare to endure."
"Are thine ears averse to slander, child?
  Is thine heart devout and pure?

"Glad art thou in thy neighbor's joy?
  Sufferest thou his need?
Ah, then I know that thou hast seen
  The vision of My face indeed!"

A STEP ON THE STAIR

All noble visions, all sublime ideals are realized only through constant yielding of the self-life to death. We all know it superficially, but so few of us practice the truth that the way up is down. George MacDonald is the author of a poem in which he challenges a youth by telling him of a stair that leads to the stars:

Built of all colors of lovely stones,
Where no one is weary and no one moans
Or wants to be laid by.
The youth is inspired and answers,
"I will go." And the poet replies,
"But the stairs are very steep;
If you climb up there,
You must lie at the foot, as still as sleep,
A very step of the stairs.
Feet of others on you will stand
To reach the stones high piled,
But one will stoop and take your hand,
And say, 'Come up, my child.'"

The message intended is that the way to climb upward on this great heavenly stair is to become a stone, a step of the stair, on which the feet of others will press as they go upward. This is the real way to reach the shining goals of spiritual elevation which beckon us from on high.

NO EFFORTLESS SAINTHOOD

The attainment of high spiritual ideals will not be realized apart from real conscious effort. Paul said, "I strain to the things that are before." Some people try to tell us that if we have really been saved and sanctified or filled with the Spirit, high states of sainthood are from then on spontaneous, practically effortless. This teaching brings many people into bondage who, after a definite experience of salvation and sanctification, discover that it **requires much prayer, constant watchfulness, and real discipline for them to live up to their ideal of a Spirit-filled experience.** And because of this teaching that if they have really had an experience of sanctification, they will never fall below that ideal, they often cast away their confidence when they should reckon themselves dead, as Paul tells us in Romans 6. **There is no such thing as effortless sainthood. You will always be tempted in some ways to live in the flesh and to fail to walk in the Spirit.** After conversion and heart-cleansing, you will still have to be on your guard and you will probably sometimes inadvertently fail or be overtaken in a fault. Even after the definite experience of justification and filling with the Spirit, **pure sainthood will be increased and strengthened only by practice.** Some people will call me legalistic and say that I am advocating salvation by works when I say that **all goodness in living begins first in obeying rules and in keeping commandments.** True, we cannot keep Christ's commandments without a supernatural work and love in the heart, without a cleansed spirit, **but even a cleansed heart is kept clean by scrupulous, disciplined obedience.** Mozart and Mendelssohn began by running scales and striking chords, and with painful finger-exercises. To be sure, our salvation and cleansing must be wrought within before it can be worked out, but the believer is commanded to work out his salvation "with fear and trembling." **That doesn't sound like effortless sainthood to me.** Although Mozart and Mendelssohn had the music within them, they would never have become finished musicians if they had not carefully worked it out in disciplined practice according to fixed principles. The way to become skillful is to do things over and over until we can do them perfectly, without thought or conscious effort. **The way to become able to do great things is to do little things over and over again with increasing skillfulness.** This is a matter of great importance. The way to grow into mature sainthood is, after the heart is cleansed in thought, word and act, to **correct our failures so often that we finally become disciplined along lines of moral beauty and perfection.** Perhaps someone is saying, "But when I was filled with the Spirit, I didn't have to try. The thing just worked spontaneously and without effort for me." Well, I can't help wondering how much farther along you would have been if, like Paul, you had really been putting forth all the energy of your soul into straining for greater heights.

DEVOTIONS BY THE CLOCK

To become prayerful saints, we must learn to pray by the clock, at fixed times. This is very important. You will never become a praying saint if you depend upon impulse to call you to prayer. You will never become a praying saint unless you discipline yourself to a fixed program of prayer. To depend upon impulse as a guide to prayer will probably end in no praying at all. **You will have to discipline yourself to read your Bible and keep up your devotions regularly.** It is the same with all religious life. **We can only grow in patience, by using all the patience we have, clear up to the limit. We grow in patience by being as patient as we can, daily and hourly, and in the smallest matters. We become**

unselfish by practicing unselfishness whenever we have the opportunity. We grow better by striving, as Paul said, by straining to be better than we already are, and by climbing step by step toward the radiant heights of moral excellence and beauty. We become better than we are by doing better than we feel like doing, just because we know it is right. We become better by living by principle, rather than emotion.

PRACTICE MAKES PERFECT

Paul said, "I press toward the mark." That is, toward his vision and ideal. "The test of all moral life is in its tendencies." The question is not, what point you have attained, but, "Which way are you tending?" We grow always in the direction of our daily living. The powers we use develop continually into greater strength; the graces we cultivate come out more and more clearly in our character. "A bird that would not use its wings, would soon have no wings to use." And while, spiritually speaking, our soul has no wings until God gives them, those wings must be exercised in order to gain strength. Even the holy Paul, the sanctified Paul, said that he strained and pressed toward the fair vision that challenged him for the future.

CHAPTER THIRTEEN

The Veiling of the Future

As we look into the future, it is natural to wonder what it holds for us. Have you never wished that you might pull back the curtain that veils the future and take a peep into the tomorrows? Have you never wondered why God keeps the future hidden? Have you never vainly tried to open that door just as the disciples did when they asked, "Lord, wilt thou at this time restore the kingdom to Israel again?" His answer to them is His Word to all of us as we face the future: "It is not for you to know the times or the seasons which the Father hath put in his own power." This is God's plain direction to all of those who would seek to pierce that veil of secrecy by going to fortune tellers, seers, wizards and necromancers of every ilk, religious or otherwise. **God has kept the future hidden because it is best.** God sees that it is better for us to go on step by step and to live a day at a time. That is why He has promised to lead only a step at a time. "As thou goest, thy way shall be opened up before thee step by step" (Proverbs 4:12 - Free translation). Being led thus, a step at a time—living thus, a day at a time—the joys of life do not dazzle us, for our hearts have been chastened so that we have learned how to receive them. If some of us had known in advance the coming joys and prosperities, the exultation might have made us heedless of duty and of danger. We might have let go of God's hand and have grown self-confident, thus missing the blessing that comes only to simple faith. Being led a step at a time, living a day at a time, we are not overwhelmed by the sorrows of life. If we had known of the struggles and trials before us, we might have become disheartened, thus failing courage to endure. **Christ has withheld the knowledge of the future because it is better.** If you do not believe this now, sometime you will when the mists have rolled away.

THE VEILING OF HEAVEN'S GLORIES

Have you never wondered why God has not revealed more about Heaven and its glories? Perhaps that is because that revelation, if made to us now, would unfit us for duty here. A traveler tells of returning home after a long voyage in foreign lands. As soon as the sailers saw the shore of their own land, they became incapable of attending to their duties on ship. When they came into port and saw their friends on the pier, they were so overcome with their emotion that another crew had to be sent on board to relieve them. Suppose we, in this vale of tears, as we toil and struggle on in an unfriendly world, could look upon the ineffable joys of our homeland and see our friends and loved ones beckoning us from that safe shore, do you not think it would make us incapable of performing our duties? Do you not think that the vision of its splendors would so charm and entrance us that we should weary of earth's painful life? If we could see our loved ones in that fair land, would we be content to stay here and finish our work? **Surely it is better that more has not been revealed.** The veiled glory does not dazzle us, and yet faith has sufficient knowledge to sustain it **until at last the morning breaks. It is better for us that the future is veiled and revealed to us only a step at a time.** We may wait in patient faith when mysteries confront us, or when shadows lie across our pathway, confident that while we do not know the way we go, we know our Guide, and He withholds that knowledge only because it is best.

"AS THY DAYS, SO SHALL THY STRENGTH BE"

It is really a mercy that we do not get life in a whole piece, but only a day at a time, for then we never have more than one day's battles to fight, or one day's work to do, or one day's burdens to bear, or one day's sorrow to endure. **God has a reason for breaking life up into small units and dealing it out a day at a time.** In the wilderness, God never gave His chosen people more manna than one day's portion at a time, except on the morning before the Sabbath. He positively forbade them to gather more than one day's supply at a time. This was God's way of teaching His people to live a day at a time and trust Him for tomorrow. To them He gave the all-sufficient promise, "As thy days, so shall thy strength be" Deuteronomy 33:25. Strength was not promised in advance—enough for all of life, or even for a year, or for a month—but the promise was that for each day, when it came with its own needs, duties, battles, and griefs, enough strength would be given. As the burden increased, more strength would be imparted. As the night grew darker, the lamps would shine out more brightly. The important thought here is that strength is not emptied into our hearts in bulk—a supply for years to come—but is kept in reserve, and given day by day, just as the day's needs require.

A DAY AT A TIME

Life is like a school in which one lesson well learned prepares us for the next, but only for the next. Going through life, living a day at a time, is like traveling by the light of a lantern. It lights the path only a single step in advance; but when that step is taken, another is thereby lighted, and so on, until the end of the journey. It is thus that God lights our pathway. He does not show us the whole of it when we set out; He makes one step plain, and then, when we take it, another, and then another. "As thy days, so shall thy strength be" Deuteronomy 33:25. We are safer this way.

SHOES FOR ROUGH ROADS

These words are a part of a promise given to the tribe of Asher. This tribe was given a rugged, mountainous section of the land. That meant that they would have rough roads to travel. Common sandals made of wood or leather would not endure the wear and tear of the sharp, flinty rocks. There was need for some special kind of shoes. Therefore, God placed iron in those rugged hills, a provision for iron shoes needed to travel the rocky pathways. This was what God meant in the promise "Thy shoes shall be iron and brass, and as thy days, so shall thy strength be."

This promise is meant for all who travel rugged pathways. And that means all who are, like Paul, straining toward the things that are before. If you really mean to climb, you will need strong, tough shoes, for the way up is never smooth and easy. But God has promised us all, that in this business of spiritual mountain climbing, He has provided suitable shoes.

Asher's portion was not an accidental one; it was of God's own choosing. Nor is there any accident in the ordering of the place, the conditions, the circumstances of any child of God. All is ordered for the best development of each individual.

LIFE'S FINEST GOLD

Although Asher had been placed in a rough country, God had placed iron in the hills to provide rugged shoes for the rough roads. The same law rules in all of God's providences for His children. When we get to the rough country, we will find the iron for rugged shoes. We often wonder how we are going to get through certain anticipated trying experiences. We are tempted to worry and fret over what we feel is our lack of grace to meet trials which we anticipate may come. That is because we fail to grasp the significance of this promise. **God does not promise strength for needs while those needs are still future.** God does not put strength into our arms today for battles tomorrow. God does not provide iron for heavy shoes until the rough country is reached. **But when the conflict is upon us, then the strength comes.** When the mountainous country is reached, then the ore for iron shoes is found. But there is no assurance of strength to bear great burdens when there are no great burdens to be borne. Help to endure temptation is not promised when there are no temptations to be endured.

People sometimes worry and fret because they feel they do not have dying grace. But dying grace is not promised, nor needed, while it is still our duty to live.

All of my life I wondered how I could ever live if my mother were to be taken. But when at last that day came, I had one of the greatest surprises of my life. Never before had I experienced such conscious comfort. I shall never forget it.

We may be sure that if God directs our pathway over rough and rugged ways, it is for our own discipline and development. In the rugged hills of toil and testing, life's finest gold is found.

GOD GUIDES THE PLANETS

In the coming year, the pathway ahead of us is veiled in mystery. But we need not fear if we can be sure that our own way will be divinely directed. Many people find it difficult to believe in divine guidance. They know He guides suns and stars in their orbits so carefully that they never wander a hair's breadth from their course. They know that He directs planets so accurately that in all the vast universe, with its millions of worlds, with its system upon system and system above system, there is absolute precision in all of their movements age after age. No star is ever too fast or too slow. No planet ever leaves its orbit. The sun is never late rising. God has marked out paths for the worlds and He causes them to move in these paths. So exactly does He guide them that scientists can calculate the exact moment of an eclipse, thousands of years in advance.

HE ALSO GUIDES HUMAN LIVES

But does God interest Himself in anything so small as the individual lives of men? If He does give direction, is it confined to the careers of great men who carry important destinies in their hands and who are sent on missions of far-reaching responsibility, or does He give thought to the daily path of each of the millions of His children? Does He show a little child the road through the bewildering tangles? Does He guide a wandering one home? **We can conceive that He might direct the career of certain great men whose lives are important to the world; but will He show common people the way?** Will He guide a poor man or a little child? He calls the stars by their names, but does He know who I am?

HE GUIDES HIS LITTLE ONES

The Scripture provides abundant answers to these questions. For example, we are told that God is our Father. What are the characteristics of fatherhood? Is there anything so small in the lives of children that their father is not interested? **All that is good in human fatherhood is only the reflection of the divine.** We are told not only that He calls the stars by their names, but that the Good Shepherd calls His own sheep by name. If he feeds the sparrows and clothes the lily, we may be sure that He will instruct one of His children in the way which he should go. Let no one think that he is only one of a crowd in God's thought. **Each believer has his own place and is cared for just as if he were the only one. God loves us as individuals.** God's will takes in the smallest events in life. God's hand is in every event. Nature is under God's control. Nothing in nature takes place by accident. No storm, no earthquake, no cyclone or tidal wave ever takes place without His permission. Even the snowflakes are under His control. The sea is His and He made it. He says to the proud waves, "This far and no farther" Job 38:11. **This world is not controlled by chance, nor by any blind fate, but by Him who loved us and gave Himself for us.** "The hands that were pierced do move the wheels of human history and mold the circumstances of individual lives" (Maclaren). If all of this is true, we may be sure that we shall not be left to find our way alone.

HE GUIDES BY LITTLE THINGS

If we are not careful, we may fail to recognize God's guidance, for His leading often takes us along homely, commonplace ways. **We are in danger of associating God's leading only with the more dramatic, unusual, or thrilling things of life.** But if God's leading were confined only to great or outstanding moments or events, life would be quite empty of Him, for big events are rare. Unless we are able to recognize God's leading in the daily humdrum routine, we may probably miss it altogether. **We must remember that great principles are as truly exercised and strengthened by practicing them in commonplace circumstances as in those which seem more sensational.** Please don't forget this. It is a truism. God's leadership is as uninterrupted in the routine affairs of lowly service as it is in the so-called sensational events of a public character. **Although your life is largely hidden, this does not mean that God takes less pains with you than He does with those who live in the limelight.** Deep in fathomless ocean caves bloom flowers of rarest perfection and beauty. Although they are never seen by human eye, God has taken just as much pain with them as with those flowers that bloom in the greenhouses and gardens.

EARTH'S CRAMMED WITH HEAVEN

The humblest lot affords room enough for the noblest living. We may feel that this is not really true. There are so many duties in our lives that are irksome. Young people find their schoolwork dull. There are faithful mothers who grow weary of the endless duties of the household. There are good men who tire of the routine of office or store or mill or farm. There comes to most of us, at times, the feeling that what we have to do day after day is not worthy of us. We feel that we must have been made for nobler things. **But right in the very duties which you might naturally disdain, you will find the opportunity to develop noble character.** Remember that it was while Moses was tending sheep at the backside of the desert that he saw the vision of the bush that burned. If he had been like some of us in our daily tasks, he probably would have missed that vision. "Earth's crammed with heaven and every common bush afire with God."

HE GUIDES THROUGH COMMONPLACE THINGS

God is found usually in the most unlikely places. It was to the lowly shepherds on the hillsides of Judea that the blessed proclamation was given, and they found God, not in earthly palaces, but in a common stable. They might have missed God's guidance if they had not been occupied with lowly tasks. It was while Gideon was threshing grain and Elisha was plowing with oxen that their revelations of God were given. Often it is in the lowliest ways that God is found.

Philip said to Jesus, "Show us the Father," and Jesus' answer shows His disappointment. "Have I been so long time with you and yet hast thou not known me, Philip? He that hath seen me, hath seen the Father" John 14:9. Philip evidently thought that revelation should be one of splendor and had failed to recognize the Father in the quiet of the everyday life of Christ. Christ usually is revealed to us in plain garb and in lowly ways. We decline tasks and duties that are assigned to us, thinking they are beneath us, not realizing that they have been given to us by God and that angels would eagerly perform them. Evidently not one of the disciples would take the basin and towel that last night and wash the feet of the others and of the Master. Washing the feet was the humblest of all tasks. The lowliest slave in the household did it. But while these men thought it was beneath them to do such a menial task, the Lord of heaven and earth took the towel and did it. **He did not consider it beneath Him.**

CHAPTER FOURTEEN
What Is Your Mission?

Suppose Paul had lost confidence in God's guidance while he was in prison. He would never have received the revelation of divine truth with which he was entrusted. Much of the truth that has thrilled the souls of millions was unfolded to Paul while he was making tents. **Many of us never have learned to see God in our everyday life.** If Jesus "regulates the universe by the mighty power of his command" (Hebrews 1:3, TLB), He must also be regulating my daily duties. It seems to us that our life is not worthy of us, that its splendor is lost in our commonplace tasks. We think that we could find God in life if we occupied some conspicuous place, or could perform some sensational task, or could travel in distant places. **But no occupation is in itself lowly. We should not feel humiliated by our earthly condition. It all depends upon what our mission is, not our occupation.** Jesus was a carpenter by trade, **but that was not His mission.** You may be a grocer, or a butcher, or a farmer by occupation, but if you are all-out for God, your mission is the same as the preacher or the song leader or the evangelist or even of Christ Himself, to establish the Kingdom of God. **It is your mission and not your occupation that exalts or degrades you. When the mists have rolled away, we shall see that the scrubwoman whose mission is to exalt Jesus Christ is far more glorified than the princess who is living for self. God is in all life of which He is the center.**

CHEATED IN LIFE?

Perhaps you have felt that you have hardly had a fair share of life's opportunities and privileges. You have been fretting because others seem to be more highly favored than you. You have been discontented and depressed. Maybe that is the reason you have missed the sense of God's guiding in your life. Many years ago a young lady in our congregation had a very sad face. She was dissatisfied and unhappy. Her outlook seemed dark. There was little to brighten her life. She felt that she had been cheated in life. She did not have a Christian home and background. She was not beautiful nor talented. She didn't know where she could fit. She thought our children should be happy because they had every opportunity for development which she had been denied. It was easy to understand why they should be happy. She found it difficult to get victory over bitterness in her heart. But one day she obtained inner release. She was filled with the Spirit. Soon she lost her gloom and became radiant.

I watched her begin to grow. Her lot seemed unchanged, but she was changed inside. And then one day she told me, with beaming face, that she had found her place, her calling in life. This was thirty-five years ago. Today she has completed almost thirty years of illustrious service on a foreign mission field. Perhaps you think there are no miracles anymore—but when life is Christ-centered, and all that we do is done for Him, all life becomes aflame with God. All life becomes a miracle just as truly as the life of any Bible saint. *If your life is God-centered, it is just as sacred as that of a minister or a missionary and has just as much of God in it.*

THINK OF CHRIST'S LOWLY SPHERE

Think of Jesus for a moment. At twelve years of age He went up to the temple, and there He became the center of attraction as He confounded the doctors of the law and other religious authorities. But what did He do when His mother found Him and gently chided Him? He went back to His lowly peasant home in Nazareth and was subject to His parents. There in those humble surroundings, while He worked in a carpenter's shop, He found scope enough for the development of the richest nature the world has ever seen and for the fullest and most complete duty ever exemplified. **Therefore, however dull our task, however dreary our duty, however limiting our circumstances, we may be assured that they afford full opportunity for the highest development of noble character.** And we may be assured our hardest toil, our most irksome tasks, our lowliest duties and most uncongenial surroundings will in no sense deprive us of Christ's guidance, **since He Himself lived under the discipline of just such con-**

ditions. Let us not miss His guidance because we cannot see Him in common things.

GOD'S WAYS ARE RIGHT BUT
NOT ALWAYS SMOOTH

We are also in danger of failing to recognize God's guidance because the ways in which He leads are not always smooth. It is natural for us to think that if God is leading, our way will be easy and delightful. But such is not the case. In Matthew 4:1 we read, "Then was Jesus led up of the Spirit into the wilderness to be tempted of the devil." Then God does sometimes so order our lives that we are carried into places where the moral fibre of our character is put to the test. And that means that Satan will sometimes be turned loose upon us. That means rough and rugged ways; that means mystery, darkness and pain. **When God leads us into certain pathways we expect them to be tranquil and we are surprised and sometimes petulant and peevish when we discover it to be otherwise. We are in danger of questioning His leading because the pathway is rough.**

PAUL'S UNEVEN PATHWAY

Take for instance Paul's journey to Rome. If he had been under the impression that God's leading was always in smooth paths, he would have decided before he got very far that he had completely missed God's guidance. For months he was confined in lonely dungeons, a prisoner of Rome. Then, instead of being carried on a heavenly chariot, he was left to toss upon a stormy sea, to pass through days of hopelessness and nights of despair, when for fourteen days no one could eat, and then finally to suffer shipwreck. And how did he get to land? There was no heavenly galley to take him off, no angel form to still the raging sea, **no supernatural sign that he was in God's will.** Just like all the rest, Paul had to seize a spar and swim out the best he could. I imagine he didn't feel very romantic about that time. I imagine that he could easily have listened to Satan whispering that this was a pretty way for a servant of God and an Apostle of Christ to fare. Listen to his testimony:

> **I have been often at the point of death;** five times have I had forty lashes (all but one) from the Jews, three times I have been beaten by the Romans, once pelted with stones, three times shipwrecked, adrift at sea for a whole night and day; I have been often on my travels, I have been in danger from rivers and robbers, in danger from Jews and Gentiles, through dangers of town and desert, through dangers on the sea, through dangers among false brothers—through labour and hardship, through many a sleepless night, through hunger and thirst, **starving many a time,** cold and ill-clad, and all the rest of it. And then there is the pressing business of each day, the care of all the churches (2 Corinthians 11:24-28, Moffat).

If Paul had expected God's leading to be only in calm and easy ways, he would have missed it altogether. But he did not miss it. Under these very circumstances, he testified, "Wherever I go, thank God, He makes my life a constant pageant of triumph in Christ."

Here is God's pattern for our lives. Here is the assurance that God leads people who have to face difficult circumstances and walk rugged ways. **God's leading does not necessarily lift us above the common plane of ordinary existence. It may lead us over very uneven ways, even as it did Paul.**

BEAUTY OUT OF DARKNESS

We are told that in one of the famous lace shops of Brussels there are certain rooms devoted to the spinning of the finest and most delicate lace patterns. These rooms are altogether darkened except for the light from one very small window which falls directly upon the pattern. There is only one spinner in the room, and he sits where the narrow stream of light falls upon the threads of his weaving. "Thus," the guide says, "do we obtain our choicest products. Lace is always more delicate and beautifully woven when the worker himself is in the dark and only his pattern is in the light."

May it not be the same with us in our weaving? Sometimes we, too, work in the dark. We cannot understand what we are doing. The pattern is all very vague to us. And yet some day we may discover that the most exquisite work of our life was done in those periods of darkness. The very path which seems so dark, so hard for our feet, is the path God is choosing. "He never would send you the darkness, if He thought you could bear the light."

CHAPTER FIFTEEN

Life Is Not All Activity

The writer of the Shepherd Psalm voiced this truth when he said, "He maketh me to lie down." **Life is not all activity, work, service.** While it is true that there is no time to waste, yet we are not to be forever pressing on in the sense of being always outwardly active. **Sometimes God may ask us to stop and lie down awhile.** Naturally, we do not care to lie down. We would much rather keep on our way. We are loath to tarry. We think it is a loss of time to turn aside and rest awhile. **It seems to us that a minute not filled with activity is a minute wasted.** We have not yet learned that sometimes we might make better progress by lying down than by pressing on. So we often fret and chafe when we are compelled to lie down for awhile.

TIME SPENT IN SICKNESS
NEED NOT BE WASTED

Some of us think we would almost sin if we were to rest even a few hours in our busy week. We have so cultivated the sense of responsibility that we feel it is wrong for us to be inactive. **But there is danger that we may overlook the need of being fed ourselves if we are to feed others.** It is easy to forget that we need to be blessed before we can be a blessing. **The day that does not get its quiet time with the Master has been a lost day.** Whenever the Good Shepherd makes us lie down, we can be sure that it is in order to give us some new blessing. This is true many a time when He leads us into a sick room and draws the curtains upon us. **He does not intend the days or weeks we spend there to be wasted.** The outward activity in which we are engaged, the worldly affairs in which we are employed are not by any means the only work of life, **nor the most important.** We are not here merely to plow and sow and reap, to build houses or bridges, to keep books or set type, to manufacture or buy and sell and get gain. These occupations may be right enough, **but our main purpose here is to grow into the character and likeness of Christ. That is learning agape love. All of these other activities are incidental. The making of Godlike character is God's real objective.** We are in danger of forgetting this when we are called away from our common occupation for a longer or a shorter period of time. It is doubtless because there is something that needs to be done **in us**, something that is more important than the work we would do if we were to continue uninterrupted at our tasks.

If we could know this when we are made to lie down, it would help us to be more patient and obedient. There is a blessing awaiting us in the quiet room into which we are led. Our theology may question this but there is a lesson assigned which we must now learn. As a songbird is shut up in a dark place to learn a new song which it could not have learned in the light, so in our withdrawal into the shadow we are to be taught some new sweet song in the night which we may sing ever after in the ears of sad and weary ones. And no price is too great to pay for the privilege of learning to sing even a single note which will bless the world. (Adapted from J. R. Miller)

A man lived fifty years—joy dashed with tears;
Loved, toiled, had wife and child, and lost them; died;
And left of all his long life's work one little song
That lasted—naught beside.
Like the Monk Felix's bird, that song was heard;
Doubt prayed, faith soared, death smiled itself to
* sleep;*
That song saved soul. You say the man paid stiffly?
Nay, God paid—and thought it cheap.

No sorrow is too great to endure if it reveals to us some new beauty in Christ or develops in us some new Christlike disposition. Since the best of all friends is Jesus, may it not be worthwhile to drop all our tasks for a time in order to get into closer, sweeter, and more intimate fellowship with Him?

I am preaching to myself now. Life would come to mean a great deal more to us if we would learn to take it more leisurely. We are under such pressure much of the time that we do all of our work in a feverish way. We make such a clatter in our rushing haste that we **cannot hear the still, small voice.** We hurry so that we have no time to think, to meditate, to get acquainted with our Master. The secret of John's beautiful character was his lying in the bosom of Jesus, but we are too rushed to spend time that way. And so, God must sometimes call us aside to rest awhile and make us lie down.

THE IMPORTANCE OF "RESTS"

Ruskin wrote the following to a young woman correspondent: "There is no music in a rest, Katie, that I know of, but there is the making of music in it." It is the same in life as with music. The rests on the music staff in one sense are not a part of the music. Yet they are as important in their place as if they were notes to be played or sung. It would spoil the harmony and rhythm if a careless player or singer were to disregard the rests. May it not be that the rests which God imposes are quite as important in the melody of life as any of the notes on the staff? To overlook them or to fill them up is to mar the music. And so God's leading may not always be in paths of activity. It may sometimes lead us into quiet resting places. "In quietness and confidence shall be your strength" Isaiah 30:15. The Apostle Paul exhorts the Thessalonians to study to be quiet. And that does not come easily. **Patience is one of the greatest, if one of the scarcest, virtues.** If you doubt this, look for the word in your concordance. There are moments and hours in life when the supreme duty is to do nothing, to stand quietly, waiting for God to work or the time to come when we can act. Sometimes we are so impatient that we must be compelled to take rests in our busy life. We are in the midst of rapid movement, hurrying on with great eagerness, when suddenly we find a rest written on the staff. Because we are in too big a hurry and we disregard it, fail to take it voluntarily, God sometimes must compel us to take it.

He may have to disable us for a time, in order to get us to mind the rests in the melody of life. We really need these rests to make the harmony of life full and rich. Sometimes God can get them into our lives only by **compelling** us to take them.

EVERY LIFE NEEDS ITS WINTERS

Nature teaches us the necessity for periods of inactivity. Winter arrests the growth of vegetation. The long months when there are no leaves and no fruits seem to be time lost. But we know that winter is no mistake and that the time is not lost nor wasted when the tree is resting. It only gathers its forces for the next year's growth and fruitage. Every life also needs its winters when everything seems to stop, but there is not necessarily any loss in the quiet waiting.

> *In every life*
> *There's a pause that is better than onward,*
> *Better than having or mightiest doing;*
> *'Tis the standing still at sovereign will.*
> *There's a hush that is better than ardent speech,*
> *Better than sighing or wilderness crying;*
> *'Tis the being still at sovereign will.*
> *The pause and hush sing a double song*
> *In unison low and for all time long;*
> *O human soul, God's working plan*
> *Goes on, nor needs the aid of man!*
> *Stand still and see!*
> *Be still and know.*

"The Lord's blessing is our greatest wealth. All of our work adds nothing to it" Proverbs 10:22, TLB. Not all of us understand this. It contradicts our theology. But if we live long enough we may discover our error. This author has reason to know.

GOD IS BEATING TIME

If only we understood God better, we would see that the rests which God writes into the bars of our life are necessary to make the music perfect. We think that we have lost time when we are compelled to be inactive through sickness or old age. But not necessarily. The passive duty of the sick days, when we are shut away from the hurrying world, the duty of being quiet and patient and trustful, may sometimes be quite as sacred and important as are the urgent duties of the days of health and youth.

How does the musician read the rests? See him beat the time in unerring count and catch up the next note true and steady as if no breaking place had come between. Not without design does God write the music of our lives. Be it ours to learn the time and not be dismayed at the rests. They are not to be slurred over, are not to be omitted, are not to destroy the melody, nor to change the key note. If we look up, God Himself will beat the time for us. It is not ours to write the score; it is ours only to play or sing as God has written it. We have no right to change a note or a point, to insert a rest or omit one. We must play it exactly as it is written.

When in life we come to rests which are written for us into the Great Composer's score, we should consider them just as much a part of the music as are the notes on the bars. We need not complain of the loss of time in illness, in forced leisure, in frustrated efforts, nor fret that our voice had to be silent, our part missing in the music. There is no real loss in these breaks or pauses, if we take them as a part of the Master's plan. We do our duty best by not trying to do anything when God bids us be still. We need not fret that we cannot be active for God when God clearly does not want us to be active. A woman who had learned the secret of submission and peace and meaning of the rests, demonstrated an amazing submission and faith when she said, "I hear God saying to me, 'Lie here and cough.'" While that may seem contrary to the teaching of Divine healing, and maybe that woman did not have the light on that subject which some of us have, yet that submission and faith may have been, in her case, a necessary prerequisite to faith for her healing. And even if she never exercised faith for healing, the submission and faith which enabled her to make such a statement is probably of more value in God's sight than a faith which could remove mountains but which had not yet learned that secret of submission. The life which pleases God most is one which takes the music as God writes it without question, believing in His love and His wisdom and sure that He is right. (Adapted from J. R. Miller)

In the grand oratorios of life
God writes us unexpected rests.
These break the rush, the strain, the storm, the strife,
And are our surely needful tests!

DEVOTION BEFORE ACTION

Because of the mistaken idea that we serve God and make spiritual progress only through outward service and activity, our devotional life of this day is sorely neglected and God's cause and our personal experience suffer loss. Because of this, the ways in which God leads are not always ways of activity; they may be ways of enforced stillness. "Every true Christian life needs its daily silent times, when all is still, when the busy activity of the other hours shall cease, and when the heart, in holy hush, shall commune with God. One of the greatest needs in Christian life these days is more devotion."

PRIORITY OF DEVOTION

Not many of us know this, but our devotional life is the most important part of our relationship with God. We are talking now about time alone with God, when we do nothing else but wait upon Him. We are not thinking about praying as we go, as we work or as we do something else. All of this is possible and necessary. Everyone should do this. But the King of kings deserves more than this. He communicates His will and shares His secrets only with those who are willing to "take time to be holy" and to share time alone with Him, to be quiet enough to hear His voice. Would God plead so many times in His Word for us to wait for Him unless He had something important to say to us or do in us? See how often the word "wait" is in your concordance.

Personal familiarity with the Word and time alone with the Lord is more important than all other spiritual occupations combined. You don't have to accept this, but in my opinion it is more important than public worship, mutual fellowship with the Body, listening to preached sermons, attending Bible classes, hearing taped messages, engaging in personal evangelism, even making financial contributions. All of this is very important. None of it should be discounted. But I am personally convinced that your devotional life is the most essential thing to the preservation and effectiveness of all other worthwhile spiritual activity. Neglect your devotional life and all other spiritual relationships will suffer.

Ours is more an age of work than an age of prayer. The tendency is to action rather than to worship; to busy toil, rather than to quiet sitting at the Savior's feet to commune with Him. The keynote of our present Christian life is devotion to active service, but devotion to the Person of God, Jesus Himself, is the very root of effective activity.

Before there can be a strong, vigorous, healthy tree, able to bear much fruit, to stand the storm, to endure the heat and cold, there must be a well planted and well nourished root; and before there can be a prosperous, noble, enduring Christian life in the presence of the world, safe in temptation, unshaken in trials, full of good fruits, there must be a close weld with God in secret. **We must receive from God before we can give to others,** for we have nothing of our own with which to feed men's hunger or quench their thirst. We are but empty vessels at the best, and we must wait to be filled before we have anything to carry to those in need. We must listen at heaven's gates before we can go out to sing the heavenly songs in the ears of weariness and sorrow. Our lips must be touched with a coal from God's altar before we can become God's messengers to men. We must lie much upon Christ's bosom before our poor earthly lives can be struck through with the Spirit of Christ, and made to shine in the transfigured beauty of this blessed life. **Devotion fits us for activity.**

In order to get this preparation for usefulness and service, we all need to get into the course of our lives many quiet hours, when we shall sit alone with Christ in personal communion with Him, listening to His voice, renewing our wasted strength from His fullness, and being transformed in character by looking into His face. Busy men need such quiet periods of spiritual communion, for their days of toil and care and struggle tend to wear out the fibre of their spiritual life and exhaust their inner strength. Earnest women need such silent times, for there are many things in their daily household and social lives to exhaust their supplies of grace. The care of the children, the very routine of their home life, the thousand little things that try their patience, vex their spirits, and tend to break their calm, all of these make it imperative that every Christian woman get into her life at least one quiet hour every day, when, like Mary, she can wait at the feet of Jesus and have her own soul calmed and fed. Too many of us give to God only the fag end of our day. (Adapted from J. R. Miller)

This message opened with the emphasis on action. It closes with the emphasis on devotion, for there can be no action that is effective in the spiritual realm, without devotion. This thought has been most sufficiently expressed by S. D. Gordon in *Quiet Talks on Prayer*: "You can do more than pray after you have prayed. But you cannot do more than pray until you have prayed."

THE KOREAN PRAYER MOUNTAIN

The average American believer has seldom taken prayer seriously. We know little about making "prayer the main business of life." In fact, few of us have probably ever even thought of such a thing. Many of us have a sneaking notion that prayer is a waste of time. We think we cannot afford to take the time to pray. We have too much to do. We think only invalids, retired, or retarded people are the ones who should do that.

This is because we do not believe that **"prayer is where the action is."** The church at large has failed to comprehend spiritual reality. Satan has kept us blinded to the fact that the real world is the spirit world, and that the fact that spirits do not have visible bodies does not mean that they are nonexistent. In Ephesians Paul explains that spirits are genuine personalities and have all of the identifying characteristics of a person except a visible body. Although they are imperceptible to vision as air and electric current are, yet they are just as real. Spirits are the actual manipulators of human personalities and the social order in general, even though we are unaware of it.

This is why Paul said, "For we are not fighting against people made of flesh and blood, but against persons without bodies—the evil rulers of the unseen world, those mighty satanic beings and great evil princes of darkness who rule this world; and against huge numbers of wicked spirits in the spirit world" Ephesians 6:12, TLB.

Notice that these personalities function in the world's social order. They rule the community of people. They are called "great evil princes of darkness who rule this world." Evidently they are innumerable, probably numbering in the millions, even billions, because Paul says there are "huge numbers" of them.

They are under Satan's leadership and operate entirely to promote his diabolical desires, aims, and purposes. They are in constant opposition, enmity, and conflict with God and with everything holy. There is never a moment when they are not seeking to "kill, steal, and destroy." John says that "we know the whole world is under the control of the wicked one" 1 John 5:19.

Satan and his hierarchy are not independent spirits. God is using prayer as on-the-job-training for rulership following the Marriage Supper of the Lamb. Therefore, by a special, exclusive, constitutional decree, He has delegated authority to the members of His Body over all the power of the enemy. This authority to bind and loose evil spirits is with the promise that "nothing shall by any means hurt you" Luke 10:19.

As far as I know, only redeemed human beings have been given this blanket order to bind and loose Satan in earthly affairs (Matthew 16:18, 19 and 18:18). This is because God is using Satan to teach the church overcoming in preparation for the throne (Revelation 3:21). Since this is true, Satan will be bound and loosed in earthly affairs only to the extent that redeemed humanity exercises its God-given authority. This is why **prayer is where the action is,** and why **prayer is the most important thing anyone can do for God or man.** This is why, as John Wesley said, "**God does nothing except by prayer.**"

We have heard about the Korean Prayer Mountain where, it is reported, ten thousand people are in prayer continuously, day and night. We are informed that out of that prayer ministry has come the largest church in the world, reminiscent of the first century Church. Is this an advance example or illustration of the fulfillment of God's prophecy and promise in Joel 2:28 and Acts 2:17 of the "pouring out of God's Spirit upon all flesh in the last days?" If so, it is a confirmation of the conviction that the fulfillment of this prophecy waits and depends upon a massive church-wide revival of intercessory prayer. Although God has spoken, there is scriptural evidence that the prophecy that has gone out of God's mouth will not be fulfilled until the church takes prayer seriously and makes it her main business. Is it possible that God is compelled to use a foreign mission church to teach indulgent, ease-loving American believers that the **"most important thing anyone can do for God or man is to pray"**?